"Jon Oliver's extraordinary insight into children is invaluable. He recognizes the importance of understanding child development in order to prepare today's children for tomorrow's world. *Lesson One: The ABCs of Life* is accessible and an excellent guide for parents, educators, and all who work with children."

—James P. Comer,
Maurice Falk Professor of Child Psychiatry,
Yale Child Study Center, and Dean, Yale School of Medicine

"With humor, astounding insight, and sensitivity, Jon Oliver, children's advocate, educational reformer, 'hero,' provides an indispensable guide for parents and teachers in helping children develop critical life-skills. The strategies and activities in this book for promoting self-control, self-confidence, and personal responsibility shall surely contribute toward a more civil and respectful community."

—Dr. James Fox,
The Lipman Family Professor of Criminal Justice
at Northeastern University

"A powerful book! Jon Oliver transforms lessons learned from his childhood, and from his years of experience as an educator, into a road map for making the world a better place."

—Deborah Prothrow Stith, M.D.,
Associate Dean, Harvard School of Public Health

# LESSON ONE

........................................

# The ABCs of Life

## The Skills We All Need but Were Never Taught

## Jon Oliver and Michael Ryan

*04·54*

A Fireside Book
Published by Simon & Schuster
New York   London   Toronto   Sydney

FIRESIDE
Rockefeller Center
1230 Avenue of the Americas
New York, NY 10020

For information regarding special discounts for bulk purchases,
please contact Simon & Schuster Special Sales at 1-800-456-6798
or business@simonandschuster.com

Designed by Jaime Putorti

Manufactured in the United States of America

10   9   8   7   6   5   4   3   2   1

Library of Congress Cataloging-in-Publication Data is available.

ISBN 0-7432-3792-7

With grateful permission to reprint lyrics from the following:

"The Age of Not Believing"
Words and Music by Richard M. Sherman and Robert B. Sherman.
© 1969 Wonderland Music Company, Inc.
All other Disney song references used by permission of Walt Disney Music Company.

CHILDREN WILL LISTEN, by Stephen Sondheim
© 1988 Rilting Music, Inc.
All Rights administered by WB Music Corp.
All Rights Reserved. Used by Permission.
WARNER BROS. PUBLICATIONS U.S. INC., Miami, FL 33014

HUSHABYE MOUNTAIN, by Richard M. Sherman & Robert B. Sherman
© 1968 (Renewed) EMI Unart Catalog Inc.
All Rights Reserved. Used by Permission.
WARNER BROS. PUBLICATIONS U.S. INC., Miami, FL 33014

THE ROSES OF SUCCESS, by Richard M. Sherman & Robert B. Sherman
© 1968 (Renewed) EMI Unart Catalog Inc.
All Rights Reserved. Used by Permission.
WARNER BROS. PUBLICATIONS U.S. INC., Miami, FL 33014

TIN MAN, by Dewey Bunnell
© 1974 (Renewed) WB Music Corp.
All Rights Reserved. Used by Permission.
WARNER BROS. PUBLICATIONS U.S. INC., Miami, FL 33014

YOU TWO, by Richard M. Sherman & Robert B. Sherman
© 1968 (Renewed) EMI Unart Catalog Inc.
All Rights Reserved. Used by Permission.
WARNER BROS. PUBLICATIONS U.S. INC., Miami, FL 33014

To my mom, Effie Boone

—*Jon Oliver*

To Deborah Gilbert Ryan, my lodestar, rock companion, and best friend of twenty-seven years

—*Michael Ryan*

# Acknowledgments

I would like to thank my coauthor, Michael Ryan, for his extraordinary writing talent. He puts his heart and soul into every word he writes. Michael writes for every person, and his style has a universal appeal that connects so well with the universal appeal of the ABCs of Life. Without his encouragement, dedication, and passion, this book would never have become a reality.

It has taken the skills of so many others to help Michael and me organize, write, and edit the book. The staff that I work with on a daily basis were all instrumental in getting the job done. Pamela Maulhardt used her analytical and organizational skills to turn my off-the-cuff ideas into solid concepts and create a logistical method to systematize the writing and editing process. Laura Root is a talented writer who comes through every time we are in need of a fresh perspective. She helped guide us in all creative aspects of our work. Olive Prince is so pragmatic and objective that she assures everything written about the ABCs of Life is clear, concise, and easy to understand. Fern Shamis Vona has been with the foundation long enough that she could draw from our history and multitask, utilizing her variety of talents (I call her a "Jacklyn" of all trades). I especially want to thank Fern for her seventeen years of dedication and friendship. Lesson One would not exist without her.

Lesson One would also not be in existence without the support and feedback from the countless children, teachers, parents/guardians, administrators, colleagues, friends, relatives, funders, and board members who have shared in our mission throughout our thirty-year history.

I would also like to thank John Bonner for his inventiveness and imagination in his artwork; and my agent, Carol Mann, for her vision and for believing in this project from the very beginning. In addition, I'd like to acknowledge our editor, Cherise Grant, Jonathon Brodman, and the team at Simon & Schuster for respecting our expertise and the integrity of our work, while providing assistance when needed.

Most of all, this book would not have come to fruition without the loving support, patience, and understanding of my wife, Mimi, and son, Andy. This Sherman Brothers song says it best:

*Someone to care for, to be there for*
*I have you two*
*Someone to do for, muddle through for*
*I have you two*
*. . . Could be, we three, get along so famously*
*'Cause we two have you, and I have you two, too.*

To you two I am eternally grateful.

# Contents

# 1

# Discovering Lesson One

**W**ith the world spinning out of control, how does your life become your own?"

Jon Oliver asked me that question one day some years ago; it has resonated in my mind ever since. We live as members of a society and a culture, but we are individuals, with lives of our own making. Every day we face the challenges and the joys and the difficulties of living, working, studying, and playing with others. How do you deal with people filled with rage? How do you stop beating yourself up for failure when you know you've done your best? How do you handle the everyday pressures of work and home? How do you learn to believe in yourself and work out your problems with thinking, instead of turbulent raw emotion? How do you handle life's challenges and help children handle them as well?

Where do you find the answers to these questions? Schools teach reading, writing, and arithmetic, but what about reality? What about life? If you don't learn about life's demands at home or at school, then how can your life become your own?

There's an answer to these questions: Lesson One. This unique program presents children and adults with a sequence of skills that change their lives and, someday, will change the world. These are skills, among them self-control, self-confidence, responsibility, thinking and problem solving, and cooperation, that we all need to be productive and happy. Most of us understand intuitively that we need these skills, but not all of us learn how to acquire and apply these skills.

In this book is the solution. *Lesson One: The ABCs of Life* is a practical, understandable, sequential guide for adults and kids that provides a time-tested program that has already changed the lives of thousands of children, teachers, and parents around the country.

I first discovered Jon's work at a time when the country was in turmoil over youth violence, shortly after the attacks at Columbine High School. The topic of conversation at watercoolers and coffee machines around the country was the same: What can we do about our kids? Most people thought there was no solution, that our nation's students were spiraling helplessly out of control. The prominent attorney Ty Cobb—best known for his involvement in high-profile Washington cases—wrote a poignant essay in the wake of the Columbine shootings, which asked, "How did we get so distracted and divided? Why are there so many guns and so few good public schools?" This book tries to address these issues and change our society for the better. As you read on, you will see that the lack of some basic skills can create enormous problems for individuals and for society. Without the ABCs of Life, our society's problems will only continue to grow.

One night, while listening to National Public Radio, I heard about Lesson One. I've heard a lot of explanations and prescriptions, but Lesson One seemed to be a unique voice, advocating a novel approach to address the underlying causes of the crisis in our culture. In his interview, Jon spoke about the need to begin teaching children about self-control early in life. Curious, I called him, and learned that there was far more to his program than even a thoughtful radio piece could cover. I decided to write a story about it.

In my research, I soon discovered that Lesson One was beginning to spread throughout our society. *Dateline NBC* and ABC's *World News Tonight* did major pieces about it. Jon Oliver presented Lesson One at the White House. Parents and teachers around the country were excited by the program as soon as they heard about it.

I've spent years visiting and writing about schools as a consultant for the U.S. Department of Education and as a research assistant at the Harvard School of Education, but I have rarely seen a program that made an immediate impact on the socialization and attitudes of kids—and never one as powerful as this.

At the Welch Elementary School in Peabody, Massachusetts, I first saw Lesson One in action. There was something magical about the classes that Jon taught. Children were happy and eager to participate, using their self-control and cooperating with each other. Principal Helen Apostolides later wrote me, "As a result of the program, teachers who once spent 80% of their time on classroom management and 20% on teaching, now spend 80% on teaching and 20% on classroom management. Before, we used to spend a lot of time on discipline; now we spend less time on that and more time on educating."

School by school, Lesson One changed the culture of every classroom it visited, creating climates based on mutual respect and cooperation.

I followed Jon and his staff around the country. Almost every time, school principals prepared Lesson One's staff for the worst, telling stories of bullying, playground violence, classroom disruption, and lack of cooperation. When Lesson One's staff went into the classroom, they connected with the students.

I saw its effect at schools, but I wanted to know more. I saw a satellite broadcast featuring Lesson One that was co-produced by the United States Department of Education, the Harvard School of Public Health, and the United States Department of Justice. Of the program, parent Elaine Metropolis says, "It has been very comforting for me personally as a parent to know that my daughter has those tools, these skills, her self-control and responsibility, and self-confidence. These aren't just terms that she learned that she's going to forget; they're tools that she's internalized. She can now can bring them with her. She'll have them when she goes off to college. They'll stay with her forever, just like the alphabet. You don't learn them one day and just forget them the next. You learn them and apply them to new situations." Lesson One's entertaining and sequential presentation of skills struck a chord with children and adults alike.

In the months that followed my visits, violence in our schools became an even more prominent national plague. Every time I picked up a newspaper, there seemed to be a new school shooting or a violent incident involving parents and kids at Little League or hockey games. After *Parade* magazine published an article about Lesson One, six thousand people, from every state in the country, called or wrote to learn more about what Lesson One does. The program had obviously touched a nerve. There were untold thousands of Americans out there who were eager to make a change in our society. They just needed to learn how to do it.

A basic premise of Jon's program is that most people are well-intentioned and they love and care for their children. If they treat children inconsiderately or cruelly, adults are usually just repeating behavior they learned when they were young. Because of what they grew up with, this is the perspective from which they deal with children and other adults.

It is simply human nature for us to see everything from our own perspective. However, if we limit ourselves to the perspective of our own upbringing and experiences, we risk repeating patterns because that is all we know. When we look at a very large and complex work of art, we must step back, away from our limited perspective, to see the broader picture. Once we see the big picture, we are able to move beyond the limits of our own experience. The skills help us do just that. With the skills, our viewpoints are broadened, so that we can examine each situation individually and respond in alternative ways, ways that move beyond some of the dysfunctional patterns that we are accustomed to. By using the skills, we can have the choice to stop harmful patterns and choose ones that are helpful to make our lives our own.

I've learned, through years of writing about education and family issues, that parents and other adults often think that they are preparing children for life when in fact, in some cases, they are disabling them, teaching fear and resentment instead of self-confidence, self-control, and the other skills all adults need. Pat Conroy, the author of the harrowing novel *The Great Santini*, perhaps our age's best account of how *not* to raise children, gave NPR's Terry Gross this impression he had as a child of his unforgiving and distant father: "I thought Dan Conroy would one day kill me."

As he looked back on how he became a college basketball star and a best-selling author, Conroy realized that he had picked up skills through the help and example of adults and others outside his family who helped foster his own tenacity and resilience. Like Jon Oliver, he found the skills he needed by observing and listening to many adults in his world. He was also emotionally intelligent enough to realize that his father's dismissal of his talent and his worth was not a realistic evaluation, but a product of his father's own unresolved problems.

Some people like Pat Conroy turn to teachers, neighbors, aunts, uncles, and other adults to learn the skills they need. But too many others don't. Our society must reach everyone and communicate these skills to kids and adults. We can't leave it up to chance. No matter their circumstance, all kids deserve the ABCs of Life.

Children and adults need Lesson One's critical skills to successfully and peacefully navigate their way through life. But expecting children to exercise self-control and take responsibility for their own actions without knowing basic life skills is like asking them to write a book report before they have learned how to read. For adults, it is the same as asking them to drive without understanding the rules of the road, or to swim in a pool if they have never been taught to float.

I urged Jon at the time to write a book about how Lesson One can serve as a powerful tool for helping both children and adults acquire skills that will make their lives fuller, richer, even safer. It's a tool that all people can incorporate into their lives, and I knew that Lesson One needed to do something to get the word out.

True, the world is awash in self-help books, self-improvement books, and books that claim to teach people how to live their lives, raise their children, and be happy. What makes Lesson One different?

It's a fair question, and there's a good answer to it. *Lesson*

*One: The ABCs of Life* is not a self-help book. It is the culmination of a long and exciting scientific project. Like researchers who spend years learning how to prevent the spread of polio or smallpox, Jon Oliver has devoted his life to studying how people learn—or don't learn—the lessons that will equip them for the rest of their lives. Gradually, over many years of honing and changing, the ABCs of Life were born.

This book does not present you with an arbitrary set of five keys, or ten steps, or twelve secrets to the perfect life. It is not about slogans or instant cures. Instead, you will follow a sensible plan that has earned national recognition for its effectiveness. If you read the chapters sequentially, you see how each skill builds on the ones before it; more important, you see how each one addresses a real need that our children have and how it can help effect a real change in the lives of adults as well. If our kids grow up with the ABCs of Life, they will become caring, responsible, and aware members of a civil society.

There are no supernatural powers or magic potions. The ABCs of Life are a rational, well-thought-out program that identifies the most important life skills and teaches them logically and in sequence, each one building on the one before it. The program receives glowing reviews because it approaches the issue of teaching skills in a concise, intelligible manner. More to the point, it makes learning these skills fun. It is descriptive, rather than prescriptive; engaging, not pedantic; lively, rather than academic. Fun is the secret. This book captures the spirit of excitement that surrounds the program and puts it in a form anyone, adult or child, can use.

The ABCs of Life connect to every aspect of a child's existence and, in the process, connect to adults by teaching the skills of self-control, self-confidence, responsibility, problem solving, and cooperation in ways that are accessible to children and adults alike. These skills are as basic as the alphabet; they must be treated as equally important. Just as our children crave food to nourish their bodies, they too need these skills to enrich their lives.

Changing our culture has been the aspiration of humanity for as long as history has been recorded: Shakespeare, Emerson, and Tennyson all wrote about finding a better world. Lesson One is changing lives, one child at a time. This book can dramatically change our culture by expanding the program's reach and bringing its message to a nation in need.

As you will read, Jon took the lessons of his own life as a template, then refined that model, using his experiences as a teacher, consultant, parent, and just plain human being. In his own life, as a bright, inquisitive, caring child, Jon had the same needs as any other kid—to learn how to deal with life. The intellectual and emotional support that he needed for that process did not come from his parents, who were busy professionals, so he reached out to his extended family, his teachers, his Aunt Fran and his older brother Mark, and especially his beloved Effie Boone, who took this lonely kid from Brooklyn under her wing and into her heart.

*Lesson One: The ABCs of Life* defines skills simply and clearly, and makes what was intangible tangible. It will help adults teach the skills to children, and help kids experience them through unique activities and games that help them learn the skills in an upbeat and positive fashion. When grown-ups and kids collaborate on these activities, they naturally move on to discussions and stories that ground the skills in everyday life. You'll read in the following chapters about how Jon's own life experience shaped the ABCs of Life. Also, you will learn practical ways to help you and the children in your lives have fun and learn the ABCs of Life together.

Every year, at my house, a pair of small birds called phoebes builds a nest under the eaves of the porch. The structure they create is remarkable, because the pieces they make it from are so unremarkable—a twig here, a feather there, bits of stems, dried grass clippings. I was watching them this summer and thinking that much of what they do resembles what Jon has pulled together. They know that no one source will give them all the materials they need to build the foundation for raising their offspring, so they fly about busily, finding whatever they need wherever they can, just as Jon found the elements of the ABCs of Life in many different places.

Just as Jon Oliver has done in his life and career, you should try to take your experiences, use this book in your life and the life of a child, build your own structure, and answer the most basic question that adults and children all must address:

"How does your life become your own?"

—MICHAEL RYAN

# 2

# Jon's Story— Making My Life My Own

One of the main objectives of Lesson One is to show kids and adults that learning skills for life is a positive, joyful experience. Life should be fun and exhilarating, and becoming a resourceful, responsible, resilient person—even though challenging—should be an enjoyable process. I feel strongly about this because of my personal history: For me, learning the skills was a complicated process, and the adults who should have helped most, my parents, helped me the least. Maybe you were fortunate to have adults in your life, whether parents or teachers, who were there for you. Maybe you weren't. No matter what your circumstances, my hope is that by reading my story, you will be inspired to look at your life objectively and reflect on ways to make your life and the lives of children positive and joyful.

Let me begin by explaining the title of our program. Lesson One is the name of the nonprofit company that my colleagues and I operate in Boston; it conducts programs in schools all over the country. We call it Lesson One for a simple reason: We try to teach the foundation for the lessons we all need to learn in life.

The ABCs of Life are skills we have been learning and refining for years. You'll read about them as you go along in this book; basically, they are the skills kids and adults need to have to live, learn, and get along with each other. We explain as we go how each of these skills builds sequentially on the one before it, equipping children and adults with the tools they all need for a fulfilling, productive, and happy life.

Some kids learn these skills here and there, from parents or guardians or other adults. But, in our increasingly fractured society, many children aren't getting all the skills they need in a comprehensive way. At the worst, this leads to school shootings, schoolyard violence, teen pregnancy, and drug abuse. But for many kids it simply means that they never get to reach their full potential.

Let me take a moment to tell you about how I, even though I never learned the skills from my parents, was able to find them from others around me. I want to share with you how my life experiences helped to shape the ABCs of Life and, thus, this book.

I was born in Brooklyn, New York, in 1951, ten weeks premature and weighing only three pounds, four ounces. Back then, such a premature birth and low birth weight were frightening propositions. Incubators were a new technology, and neonatology, the branch of medicine that specializes in newborns, was in its infancy. Many children in similar situations didn't survive.

While I was still hospitalized, my survival still uncertain, my parents spontaneously went off on a cruise. I found this out years later when, at my mother's funeral, one of her friends approached me and said, "I can't understand how your mother could have left you while you were still in an incubator." It never occurred to them that they needed to stay close to their ailing, newborn son while his life was in danger.

My parents had very little contact with my brother, Mark,

and me as we were growing up. They were busy professionals—he was a physician, she a teacher—and in our family, the phrase "Children should be seen and not heard" was a way of life. They bundled us off to sleepaway camp every summer from the time we were five years old so that we would not be underfoot. The most uncomfortable times I ever spent were when my parents came to summer camp on visiting day, because those were the only times I ever spent full days with them. On very rare occasions they ate dinner with us. They seldom even had conversations with us. In fact, we had to make appointments in order to see them at all.

My Aunt Fran reminded me of a time when she saw me hurrying down the street. I barely stopped to say hello, because I had an appointment with my mother. I remember that day well: Fran has always been my most loving relative, one who always listens and is there for me, but I barely said hello to her that day. A moment with my mother was a precious thing. I didn't want to miss it.

Both parents were too busy to put me to bed. My mother would be talking on the phone, keeping up with her social friends; my father would be working. Left to my own devices, I would sing myself lullabies to keep from going to sleep lonely.

Mark and I sat down one day years later and talked about our strange relationship with our parents. We tried to think of times when all four of us were together and we acted like a family. We were able to come up with only five occasions in the previous thirty years.

On these few family outings, we went to see movie musicals or Broadway musicals. The screen and the stage presented me with a romanticized version of family life; each of the shows ended with a vision of optimism and hope. To this day, I connect my memories of the family outings with these exhilarating feelings. So throughout this book, you will find countless references to these things, these bits of entertainment that helped me hold on to the optimism and hopefulness that these happy, fictional worlds presented—and that my own family life didn't mirror.

My parents were nice people, well liked in the community, each devoted to a profession that made the world a little better. But they just didn't know how to be parents. They didn't understand that parenting means more than just putting a roof over your children's heads, clothing them, enrolling them in school, and counting on others to do the job of raising them. It also means equipping them with the skills that will enable them to become successful adults.

In my work today, I see many loving and caring families. Unfortunately, I also see too many families in which—because of neglect, substance abuse, job demands, or simple lack of parenting skills—mothers, fathers, and other guardians seem to assume that children will raise themselves. As you will see in this book, it doesn't work that way. If you have a child in your life—whether you are a parent or guardian, an aunt or uncle, a teacher, a friend, or even a concerned neighbor—you can help him or her gain the skills every child needs in life.

My mother was a bright, creative, sweet woman, a prodigy who skipped five grades in school, sailed through college, and became a dedicated, respected art teacher in the New York schools. Her academic talent deprived her of huge parts of childhood and adolescence and the life lessons most of us learned by going through a regular school experience. Jumped ahead of her classmates, she lost the experience of socialization most of us have while growing up with our peers, teachers, neighbors, and members of our extended family. Because of her talent and intelligence, she was treated as a sort of junior adult early in her life, at exactly the time when she most needed to experience what it meant to be a child and adolescent growing up.

Our society used to think that way, believing that childhood was a kind of necessary but annoying journey toward adulthood, and that some kids, like express trains, could be put on a fast track to get them to their destination sooner and get childhood over with as quickly as possible.

As a teacher, my mother was meticulous, hardworking, and organized. But she patterned the way she dealt with her children on her own experience of childhood. I believe that my mother was distant and seemed uncaring because nothing in her youth equipped her to sit back and have fun with her children. I came to understand that my mother's childhood experiences never helped her understand who she was on the inside.

Likewise, my father was a man of tremendous dedication with a great sense of humor. He couldn't afford to go to medical school in America, but he wanted to be a doctor so badly that he went to Germany—a country where he knew no one and was required to study medicine in a language he had to scramble to learn.

When he returned to Brooklyn and opened his practice, he became a highly respected physician in the neighborhood, the kind of authority figure family physicians were in the days before widespread specialization and managed care. "He would see patients until all hours," my Aunt Fran recalls. "He would work until two or three in the morning." My father was always on call, always available for any medical question, large or small. He did everything from delivering babies to performing tonsillectomies in the office, all with an incredibly charming bedside manner.

The problem is that raising children is also a demanding and time-consuming job, and my father felt that he didn't have the time to do it. He loved us and wanted us cared for, but he didn't want to play a role in our day-to-day lives.

By putting myself in my parents' shoes, I've come to understand more about who they were. My parents were the products of the society in which they lived. They were governed by what they thought society saw as appropriate, and they lived their lives within these narrow constraints. They never realized that they had other options, that they could make their own choices. In my life, I could have done the same thing. I could have let my life be governed by the dysfunction of my parents. I could have wallowed in my feelings of anger, sadness, and loneliness and looked for solace in destructive habits.

Many people feel that they have no choices in their lives, that they are trapped by hurtful experiences. It's not true. We all can take control of our lives. When we internalize the skills, they help us make the choices we need to make to set our own courses and find our own directions. By reflecting on our own experiences and making the skills our own, we are preparing ourselves to share these skills with the children in our lives. Before we can help children, we have to help ourselves.

I was lucky enough to have a woman named Effie Boone in my life. She taught me that no matter what others did or said to me, I did have choices about how I was going to live my life. She gave me skills I needed to prove to myself that I could stop the pattern of family dysfunction and make my life my own. The best thing my parents ever did for us was to hire Effie, a good-natured, loving woman who came to my family two years before I was born. At first, Effie was supposed to fill in for only a week as

a receptionist in my father's medical office, which was connected to our apartment. Soon enough, she was living with us,
caring for Mark and me, making our meals, eating with us, and
taking us on excursions. Effie wasn't like anyone else I'd ever
met. She was another Mary Poppins: optimistic and full of sur-
prises, with a magnetic charm that drew people of all ages into
her loving embrace. Effie's room was a wonder, filled with
stuffed animals and toys. Her room matched the special childlike quality that I saw in her and had never seen in any other
adult. We went with her to Coney Island and Times Square, to
movies, jazz clubs, and even the Paramount Theatre. While
there, Effie visited with one of her best friends, jazz singer Dinah
Washington, while we played backstage. She was our introduc-
tion to one of the world's most fascinating cities. Effie showed us
how people had fun; we heard music that wasn't formal and
classical; we met people who didn't look like us.

Thanks to Effie, I first ate the kinds of foods many New
Yorkers love—from Chinese dim sum to Jewish deli. My parents
never took pictures of me as a child or even remembered my
birthday, but Effie always did. Effie was also the den mother for
our Cub Scout troop 471. She helped us to complete all our Cub
Scout projects and even spent all night sewing Cub Scout uni-
forms for our toy figurines. She was the only person who read to
me as a child. I can remember lying next to Effie on the bedroom
floor as she read book after book, everything from Dr. Seuss to *Dr.
Doolittle.* And she brought me my favorite flavor of ice cream—
pistachio. My parents never even knew what kind of ice cream I
liked. Effie knew my favorite ice cream because she knew me.

With Effie's help, I made it through my first day of kindergarten. Leaving home, going out of the only world I'd ever
known to spend a day with complete strangers in an environ-

ment I didn't understand, was frightening to me. But I was also afraid that my parents would forget about me and leave me while I was away at school. Effie took my hand and walked the seven blocks with me to ease my fears. On my journey to the un-known world of kindergarten, Effie promised me that she would be there for me no matter what. In addition, Effie promised me a trip to Coney Island as a reward for getting through the first day. Sure enough, at the end of the day, Effie was waiting in the schoolyard. She made good on the promise of Coney Island that day, and we went to Nathan's for hot dogs and french fries, rode on the Wonder Wheel, and had pistachio ice cream. Her uncon-ditional love surrounded me throughout my childhood. And knowing that she was there that day helped me to deal with all my fears.

Effie's love showed me the joy in celebrating holidays. She took us to her relatives' homes for Thanksgiving dinner, a glow-ing, raucous affair with her extended family. In addition to cele-brating Hanukkah, we celebrated every Christmas with Effie. My brother and I spent hours decorating the artificial tree that stood tall in our apartment. As Effie put the tinsel up strand by strand, Mark and I marveled at the sparkling colors on the tree, and when we were finished we sat with Effie under its festive glow. Afterward, we fell asleep in Effie's arms as we watched the Christmas specials on TV. And sure enough, some special toy that we had pointed out to Effie in the local toy store was always lovingly wrapped and waiting for us under our tree on Christmas morning.

Most of all, Effie taught me about people. She let me know—in no uncertain terms—which of my parents' social-climbing friends were phonies. She took note of the people who came to "chat" with my father as a friend but were really looking for free medical advice. Effie turned these situations into lessons about people and life. She explained people's motivation for honesty, sincerity, or cruelty. Effie taught me to look at the inside of people rather than judge them by their outside appearance. She taught me that what was important was the nature of a person's heart. Effie tried to make sure that we were surrounded by people who provided us with unconditional love. She arranged for us to spend Friday evenings with Grandma Bertha, Aunt Fran, and Uncle Leon, and my cousins Stu and Lori. At their homes we were nourished with homemade chicken noodle soup and love. They really cared about us; they treated us as humans, as important members of the family. Effie gave me the greatest gifts by teaching me what is really meaningful in life. Her lessons taught me the important things to look for in my relationships with others: being nonjudgmental, looking at things positively, valuing people for who they are, and being the best that you can be. Effie's teachings have shaped the Lesson One program just as they have shaped my life.

Sometimes when I describe Effie to people, I say that she was like a mother to us. But that isn't quite right. The truth is that Effie *was* our mother in almost every conceivable way. She didn't give birth to us, but she might just as well have. She was our source of unconditional love and support. She gave to us what our parents couldn't. As a teacher, a role model, and even a parent, Effie taught us skills that we could use for the rest of our lives. The unconditional love that was a cornerstone in our relationship with Effie provided me with a model that I have used as both a teacher and a parent. In both arenas of my life, I know that providing support regardless of what happens is one of the most powerful and transforming things a person can do.

Effie supplied me with a kind of love I never found elsewhere in childhood—a love that made no demands, knew no bounds, and was never withheld. The support I got from Effie in my childhood helped me to become the person I am today. That support gave me unique insight into how I look at relationships and situations. It gave me the passion to provide the skills to our out-of-control culture. I don't want other children to feel the way I felt in my family. I want them to be equipped with skills so that they can feel some control over their own destinies. Every day I use the lessons that Effie taught me. She helped me change my life. Just as she influenced my life, you can influence lives too.

Effie saw my imagination and creativity and thought I should go to a school that would develop my natural talents. My parents, not understanding my personality or individual needs, sent me to a prep school from the sixth grade on—not because of who I was, not because the school was a good fit with my talents or needs, but because it was prestigious. Many New York City private schools even then were notoriously competitive, focused on getting kids into the most elite universities. Because the main concern of the faculty at the prep school was what college their students would attend, I felt out of place.

Effie's influence, though, had already shaped my way of dealing with people. I was concerned about how other students and even staff members were being treated. Because I didn't feel that I fit in, I joked around and acted out to get attention. But what I really needed was someone to talk to about my feelings of alienation and insecurity, and my resentment at the school's indifference to its blue-collar employees as well as its rigidity toward its students. Okay, I wasn't Holden Caulfield, but, like the protagonist of *The Catcher in the Rye*, I wanted my school to be a better place than it was. Thanks to Effie, though, I went about changing it differently from the way J. D. Salinger's character did. Fortunately, because of Effie, I had already developed a knack for finding people who were sincere and honest to provide me with guidance.

Ralph Dupee, a man with the warm and gangly look of Stan Laurel, of the comedy duo Laurel and Hardy, was a teacher and counselor of mine in high school. He recognized early on that I felt like a fish out of water at this demanding school. In a recent conversation, he remembered me as a popular kid. "You weren't as academically successful a student as some other people," he laughed, "but you succeeded in different ways." Sometimes social class is a powerful tool of discrimination at private schools. The women who served lunch and cleaned up in the cafeteria were often treated disrespectfully by faculty and students alike. I arranged for them to dance with the fifth-graders during an assembly, at which they could feel appreciated and come to understand that they were an integral part of the school. I organized turtle races and made a film with a friend. The movie was a satire of the stuffiness of the school. Both the movie and the races were used to raise money for a scholarship fund dedicated to a teacher who had died of a heart attack.

Mr. Dupee helped me foster my creativity in these areas instead of stifling it. He taught me how to feel proud of myself rather than accept the judgments of my parents and school administrators, whose self-worth seemed dependent on getting their kids and students into prestigious colleges. Whenever I needed to talk, he was there to listen to me.

In the summers, I went to a camp in Lenox, Massachusetts, run by a man named Joe Kruger. Naturally, some kids at the camp excelled at traditional activities like archery, or canoeing, or leather crafts, but none of these was among my special skills.

In some other camps, kids who did not excel at athletics might have been shunned or ridiculed, and this can have a lasting effect, but Joe Kruger would not allow that to happen. Every week, Joe and his counselors met to discuss each of the three hundred campers. This took hours, but Joe did it anyway. By the end of the meeting, he made sure that he could find at least one thing that each child enjoyed doing. He nurtured my talent for drama, encouraging me to put on camp plays; I became a writer, director, and actor all rolled into one. Instead of becoming an outcast, I won enough respect from the staff and the kids that I was invited back for several years to work as the camp drama counselor. I will never forgot how Joe made sure that every camper was included in group activities. As you will see, it became a cornerstone of my approach to teaching the ABCs of Life. I knew from then on that I wanted to help kids find out what made them happy.

When I went back to Brooklyn, I was once again frustrated by the pretentiousness of my prep school. I wanted to deal with real people and to help them, so I volunteered at Maimonides Hospital.

The pediatric ward was often a sad place—and, unfortunately, not just because kids contracted infectious diseases or had congenital problems. At the hospital one day I saw a baby in a crib with a net around it. The child was in gruesome pain because some adult had burned the bottoms of his feet with lit cigarettes and beaten him severely. The first day I saw him, I attempted to walk right up to his crib; he cried out in fear. One of the nurses explained to me that he had been abused by a man and, therefore, had a traumatic response whenever men were around. Months went by, and every day I took a step closer to his crib. Slowly, he learned that I was not a threat to him, and I held him in my arms. Tears streamed down my face and I saw that I could make a difference in the life of a child.

I was excited about helping kids. In my junior year of high school I went to the career counselor and told him I wanted to become an elementary school teacher. He looked at me in disbelief and told me, "Men don't teach elementary school." I went home discouraged and looked through books about colleges on my own. I searched for a school that would suit my creativity. I thought it was a fact that men did not teach elementary school, so I started looking for the next best thing. I considered working in children's television or joining a children's theater company.

I decided to attend Emerson College in Boston, a school renowned for its theater and communications programs. In my first year, I studied children's theater. Pursuing my major, I tried out for the play *Ali Baba and the 40 Thieves*. I hoped to get the part of the handsome prince (we all can dream, can't we?), but I wound up getting the part of the donkey. Although I was discouraged, the best part about getting that role was that I was able to memorize my lines in one night. Sure, my only lines were "Hee-haw," but it was the presentation that counted. The play was a great success. We toured schools in the area, and my raucous "Hee-haw" antics received widespread applause. However, for some reason I felt a void. While the external reward the audience gave me felt great, I needed more. I wanted not just to entertain children but also to teach them and help them succeed in life while still utilizing spontaneity and humor.

I was at a crossroads. I didn't know how my revelation fit into my professional goals. Feeling discouraged one day, I was walking on Marlborough Street near Emerson's campus in Boston's Back Bay, when I saw a group of young kids and struck up a conversation with their teacher, Hildred Simonds, who offered me the chance to work at the John Winthrop Nursery School. Under Mrs. Simonds's influence, I slowly came to the powerful conclusion that my identity and fulfillment didn't depend on what society or my parents thought was important. I remembered the character Bert, the chimney sweep in the musical *Mary Poppins*. Even though he didn't have a job that society deemed prestigious, he took pride in his work and did it with dignity. I remembered that Effie and other people encouraged me to be myself. I decided that I really wanted to teach kids and that I was going to do just that, no matter what other people thought.

"When you came to John Winthrop," Mrs. Simonds said recently, "you just fit right in. You were a natural."

"You came in with a great sense of enthusiasm and mission," Paul Tamburello told me. Paul was already an established teacher in Brookline, Massachusetts, when I entered his classroom as a student teacher. "I think you had already formed some ideas about how to use education and how what was taught in the classroom could and should be used in kids' out-of-school life.

"In those days," Paul remembers, "the general perception was that schools taught school things. We were responsible for kids' academic life, but not much thought was given to their personal life." But we had ongoing conversations about how to nurture children socially as well as academically. We made daily plans for their academic work. Once that was finished, they had a choice of enrichment activities. It was a way to help kids feel that they were being responsible for their daily tasks and then could learn something that was more of a pleasure for them. Soon I got the chance to put some of those ideas into action.

I loved teaching; I knew it was what I was made for. It was an opportunity for me to affect kids' lives and to make a real contribution. When I was in college, I went to see the musical *Good-*

*bye, Mr. Chips.* It's the story of a dedicated teacher who takes pride in his work. In the film, the teachers and children sing the song "Fill the World with Love." They sing together about a mission that concerns not just academics but also caring and reaching out to others. I loved the idea that school and life could connect. I wanted to change the culture so that they would connect in everyone's life.

I started my professional life as a teacher in the town of Hingham, a quaint suburban harborside village south of Boston. I got all spiffed up in my new school clothes, brought unused school supplies into my first classroom, and even carried a new lunch box with me. I was ready to be a teacher. The reality of the job shocked me when one of my second-grade students, a little girl in pigtails, punched me in the back. There was no apparent reason for her to attack me, but she did it again and again, when I was at my desk or when I had my back turned to her. I didn't know what to do. They hadn't mentioned this possibility in my Methods and Materials class.

Astonished, I went into school the next day hoping it would not happen again. But this time, the young girl punched me even harder. I went home exhausted and knew I had to think of something to change this situation. Since the student was not expressing herself verbally, I assumed that this was a cry for help. The third day I went to school prepared. This time when she punched me I asked her to make a fist. With a marker I put two eyes and a mouth on her fist to create a puppet. Using her hand, she told me, "My father held a gun to me. My parents are getting divorced."

I was in disbelief that a child this young was exposed to such violence and trauma. In 1973, our society was not looking at violence and its impact on young children. But this was life. This was the reality that kids were bringing to the classroom. My first year of teaching taught me more than any Methods and Materials class ever did. During this time, the real-life drama continued to unfold in the city of Boston, where a Federal judge had ordered the public schools to desegregate. Anyone who was around in the early seventies remembers the riots, the protests, the violence and disruption that accompanied that order. My experience in the classroom combined with the tribulations of the time led me to believe I could do more. In 1974, I began working with the Boston public schools, using a very early and unpolished version of the ABCs of Life. The need was immediate and obvious.

This was also a time when the idea of integrating children in special education classes into the mainstream of school life was in its infancy. Classrooms were filled with children who had a variety of special needs, from kids who were emotionally and developmentally delayed to those who today would be considered to have attention deficit hyperactive disorder (ADHD). I was frustrated with the lack of classroom integration for kids of different needs as well as different cultural backgrounds. Kids are diverse, not just in ethnicity but also in ability, interests, and talents. I came to believe passionately that my job was to help create an environment in which they all grew to fulfill their potential. I could not stand by without at least trying to be part of the solution.

"It was a terrible time for Boston, with all the racism," Mildred Shelton remembers. She was a teacher in the Samuel Adams Elementary School in East Boston. I could tell when I met her that the last person she wanted to see in her troubled classroom was some fresh-faced young consultant. Recently, she told me I was right.

"I didn't want another program," she said. "When they told me someone was going to come in and work in the classroom, I said, 'People are coming in and out of the classroom all the time; the kids are getting confused.' I didn't want anybody else in the classroom.

"I didn't think I was interested," she said. "But as you went about explaining the program, I could see your passion. You were putting responsibility back on the kids, teaching them how to control themselves, to be in charge. I decided to give it a try, and it was wonderful. They got more confidence in themselves."

Mrs. Shelton and I, from time to time, took her students to visit a school in South Boston, a mainly white area of the city where some of the most bitter antibusing protests and violence had occurred. "We would go over to South Boston, and a first-grade class from there would come over here," she recalls. "It really worked. You were getting them used to another culture.

"I remember you had a lesson in how we all look different, but there are different colors of flowers, and they're all beautiful. If all the kids in public schools had gone through your program, we wouldn't see as much violence as we do today."

Archie Walsh, the warm, outgoing principal of the Russell School in the racially mixed neighborhood of Dorchester in the 1970s, echoed Mildred Shelton's thoughts: "At an early stage, we noticed patterns of violence in kids who were very young—kindergartners and first- and second-graders. The climate of our school really improved after you came. That year, we had more parents apply for admission for their kids than we had seats available. Parents speak to each other, and they got the word that this was a good school. I think that's largely attributable to your program."

Costella Laymon, a teacher at the Tobin School in the Mission Hill section of Boston, remembers another crucial part of what would become the ABCs of Life: "It was a fun learning time for the children, even though there was so much teaching taking place. They would be excited when you walked into the room, and smile and smile. You taught them how to use their self-control so that they could study even if there was noise all around them. That year, they learned confidence and self-respect and how to get along with each other."

That's how it all began. All through childhood, a passion for wanting to help children feel cared for and have the skills to carry themselves through life built up in me. As a young child, I never understood why my parents kept me distanced from their life. I often felt as though I were one of the children in the musical *Chitty Chitty Bang Bang*. It is the story of a land in which children were confined to dungeons while adults led their lives oblivious to the needs of their offspring. Although my parents were not a part of my life, I found that one adult could change the course of a child's life. Effie changed mine. Her love and guidance filled the gap in my life and provided me with the skills I needed to find my way. Just like Mary Poppins, Effie came to a home where the children suffered from emotional neglect, and she provided the support, structure, and encouragement that were needed.

Yet my childhood never had a Hollywood happy ending. My parents did not have a miraculous awakening in which they realized that they could be a part of their children's lives. Instead, a magnificent group of relatives, mentors, teachers, and friends built on the foundation that Effie gave me. I pieced together my life experiences, the lessons I learned from role models, and the skills I acquired in my personal and professional career. Throughout, I solidified my understanding of how skills can change the life of a child.

It is up to you and me to become an "Effie" and provide the children in our lives—students, grandchildren, Little League players, nieces and nephews, preschoolers, Girl and Boy Scouts, and of course our own kids—with the love, encouragement, structure, and positive guidance they need. Lesson One is the beginning. Understanding the skills of responsibility, self-control, respect of diversity, resiliency, problem solving, self-confidence, and cooperation at a young age helps equip children with the tools they need to survive and succeed in life.

*Lesson One: The ABCs of Life* is more than a book; it's a way of life, a way of dealing with the problems and issues we all encounter, but, most of all, it's a way of helping children. When we guide children through Lesson One and help them to internalize it, we are giving them not only the skills they need in life but also the resources to build a better future for their children.

# 3

# The Art of Living and
# Working with Kids

How do you learn to work and live with kids? When a baby is born, he or she doesn't come with a manual. There is no how-to guide. So far, we've discussed the fact that school and life often don't seem to connect; kids can graduate from grade school and high school, and can even go on to college and graduate school, while still learning very little about skills for life. Some of us can grow up without being taught anything about living or working with kids.

Isn't this one of the most important aspects of life?

Throughout human history, each generation has passed on wonderful learning and skills to the next; as the old song goes, "Generations yet unborn will teach them to their heirs." However, as our society continues to be filled with more and more violence and rage, we're learning that a lot of dysfunction has also been passed down. People are simply transmitting what they've learned. I'm not interested in assigning blame, only in breaking the cycle. Just as I learned to understand my parents' experiences and how they created the adults I knew as my mother and father, we all should reflect on and understand the experiences and influences that molded our parents. We should decide what parts of their lives we want to assume for ourselves and pass on to our children.

Our job is to learn objectivity, to learn why we do what we do, and pass on to our kids only the skills that will help them to learn and grow. This is not a matter of criticizing ourselves or those who came before us; it's a question of sorting out what will be useful and helpful for generations to come.

There are hundreds of books by "experts" that are filled with prescriptions: You don't do this and don't do that; you must do this and you must do the other thing. What we're going to do is tell you some stories from people like yourself—grandparents, teachers, coaches, parents, mentors, volunteers, and others— who've shared what's worked and what hasn't worked. We've taken all this information from around the country and put it in a practical guide to help you develop your own natural talent in passing on skills to the kids in your life.

As we get ready to teach our children the Pledge for Success, and the skills of self-control, Self-Control Time, self-confidence, responsibility, thinking and problem solving, and cooperation, it's important that we first develop our own skills. In many ways, passing on skills is an art form, a talent that, if you practice and hone it, helps you make the culture better for future generations. This chapter is about the essentials to teaching the ABCs of Life; it gets you started developing that art form and gives you the tools to refine it.

First, we talk about the impact that positive communication can have on children. Then we discuss how our voice and body language provide consistency and structure. The structure provides a boundary that makes the children feel safe and gives them the freedom to grow. We also discuss letting go. Although it's tough to do, it's necessary to help children grow and take ownership of the course of their own lives. We then emphasize the importance of sequencing skills—each one builds on the one before it—rather than trying to present a panacea, a temporary quick fix, or some trendy magic formula. In this book we show how each skill works independently but also builds on the others, just as the alphabet and the numerals come together to create communication and arithmetic.

We wrote this book as a series of stories, rather than a series of rules, to make it easier to understand and internalize. At the end of each of the following chapters, we also include a practical section, titled "Teaching the ABCs of Life"—a simple guide to help you teach each skill to children. First the skill is defined, then experienced, and then shared. People in communities around the country have told us that after learning how to use Lesson One, they were able to take what they learned and apply it to what they naturally do while living and working with kids. The ABCs of Life help them reflect on their experiences and provides an opportunity to look at their lives and the lives of those around them. By understanding the skills they need to live in a civil society, and analyzing some of the problems of our culture, they can communicate to kids the important lessons tomorrow's adults will need to make the world a better place.

## Developing Your Natural Talent

### Being Positive

"A spoonful of sugar helps the medicine go down, in the most delightful way." Mary Poppins was right—we can provide what children need while at the same time communicating the message positively. If you approach the skills with a negative tone, you create a self-fulfilling prophecy: Kids will react negatively. If you're positive and share the excitement of how the skills relate to your life, the excitement is contagious. Kids will then internalize skills that will help them survive and succeed.

In a society that often speaks in terms of good and bad, it can be easy to place a premium on winning. When we play a game, we can be so concerned about winning or losing and about our performance that we forget about the fun of playing the game and being with other people. When we get so wrapped up in the product, we can forget about the process, which is just as important. If we are doing a painting, for instance, we may get so wrapped up in the idea of what something will look like when it's done that we forget to enjoy the process of painting itself. In emphasizing the act of creating, we can think about what worked and what we can do in the future. We can focus on the positive even in difficult situations and create a foundation for future progress.

Here's an example. If a child is having a hard time learning to play the piano, you can help by first pointing out something positive about his abilities. It's important to be honest and really find things the child does well. If you're insincere, the child will see right through you. You can say something like, "You're doing a great job playing the scales, now let's work on reading the music to play a song," instead of, "What's wrong with you, why can't you read the notes?" By being positive, you give a child something to work with: translating his knowledge of the scales to reading music.

The same holds true for adults. If a spouse always neglects specific household chores, you can help change that by finding something positive about what he or she does accomplish with helping around the house. You might say, "Thanks for emptying the dishwasher. Can you please put the recyclables in the bin as well?" Think about how much more positive that is than saying something like, "I can't believe you didn't put the cans in the bin!" Labeling and judging take away from an experience; being positive sets the stage for continuous learning and growth.

But what if there's nothing positive about a situation? The movie *Pollyanna* best answers this question. A young girl, Pollyanna, earns notoriety in her town as an unfailing optimist. No matter what the circumstances, she looks at them in a positive way. After attending a fire-and-brimstone church sermon titled "Death Becomes You," Pollyanna is asked what she found positive about Sundays, the day sermons such as this occurred. She thinks for a moment, then says, "It will be six whole days before Sunday comes around again!"

No matter how dismal a situation seems, you can always find a positive. It's important to communicate these positives to the children and adults with whom we work and live. This sets the stage for developing a positive attitude and applying it to any situation that children encounter.

## Using Your Voice

Voice and body language are important in every area of life, from the classroom to the workplace to the home. I learned that years ago when I was a consultant working in Mrs. Shelton's second-grade class. A young boy picked up a chair and threatened to throw it at me. Many people's natural reaction to that sort of situation, with a child filled with rage, might have been to scream at the child. In those days, I probably would have raised my voice as well, hoping to intimidate the boy, but I was scared and totally speechless, and didn't know what to do.

But Mrs. Shelton did. Her voice went down, sounding calm

and reasonable but also commanding. Her body language—she stood firm and confident—communicated confidence, authority, and understanding. The boy slowly put down his chair and sat back in his seat. Recently she told me that she was really touched that something she did helped shape this program, but I don't think even she understands how important that moment was to developing the way we teach skills.

Soon after that incident, I was in a classroom where an angry child spat on me. My first instinct was to yell, but I quickly thought back to the experience I had with Mrs. Shelton. Suddenly, my voice went down and I said in a no-nonsense tone, "That's it." Every child in the room sat up and took note. I learned right then and there the power of the human voice.

Think about the most boring class you ever had. Michael Ryan told me about a college course he took years ago in the history of the law, which should be a fascinating subject. But it met at breakfast time—not the best time for many of us to concentrate in the first place—and the professor was a pallid fellow who never looked up from his notes, droning on and on in an uninflected monotone until Michael, on a semiregular basis, fell asleep. That's probably one of the reasons he's the coauthor of this book instead of a practicing lawyer today. For students trying to choose among a multitude of career options, a teacher who is obviously uninterested in teaching, and who makes the subject uninteresting, practically guarantees that the students will choose a profession that some other teacher makes come alive in the classroom.

Now think of the most exciting class you ever had. Was it because of the subject matter? Maybe partly. But most likely the teacher was interested, animated, and engaging—someone who varied tone and pitch and delivery, someone who could be quiet, almost hushed, and then become loud, almost boisterous. Just as a great symphony is a contrast of quiet passages and loud, grand moments, a great class touches on as many contrasting tones of voice and movement as possible. If you want your kids to learn the skills—or to learn anything else, for that matter—keep them engaged by keeping your presentation varied, interesting, and natural.

When I was studying at Emerson College, I took courses in oral interpretation. I found it invaluable to a novice educator. One of the first concepts we learned was onomatopoeia, a fancy Greek word that literally means "making the name" or "making the sound." It's actually simple. What's our word for the sound a bee makes? Buzz. Why? Because *buzzzzzz* is as close as we can come to replicating the sound.

So there we were, soon to be educators, almost adults, standing around with full-grown professors making buzzing sounds like bees. By the end of the course, I had learned some valuable lessons. I had learned not to take myself too seriously. And I learned how I could connect my voice and body language in order to keep children engaged.

Think about it. If a Highway Patrol officer pulls you over and laughingly says in a game show–like voice, "Hey, buddy, you're gonna get a ticket," will you treat her with as much seriousness and respect as the officer who, politely but firmly, says, "License and registration"? If you go to court and the judge uses a jocular tone to banter with the lawyers, will you take the proceedings seriously? On the other hand, if you go to see Jim Carrey or Whoopi Goldberg do a stand-up comedy act, will you laugh if he or she talks in the straightforward tone of a judge during the entire act? Of course not. Your voice helps convey the message you're trying to get across.

So does your body language. When communicating with anyone, it's important to be grounded. If you're off-balance, it shows. Taking a moment to plant your feet firmly on the ground helps center your voice and make your message clear. Your body can be grounded, just as your voice can be grounded. When your body is grounded, it makes the message you are communicating resonate through your entire being.

When you're trying to impart the skills to kids—whether you're a teacher or a parent or a caretaker—it's crucial to vary your voice and your movement in a manner consistent with your message. Through these experiences and observations and the feedback from teachers and parents around the country, we discovered that there are three distinct voices we can use to help us create an exciting atmosphere and a consistent set of limits. The idea is to take what you usually do and add the voices in a natural way. The voices are simply a point of reference for the way you speak and present yourself.

## Animated Voice

Use this voice when you are being playful, motivating kids to be excited about learning, or just having fun. The volume of the animated voice can vary from a whisper to an excited tone. Energetic body language coincides with an animated voice. For example, you might lean forward, use hand gestures, have an open posture, and smile with a bright and open face. The animated voice is like a roller coaster, complete with unexpected twists and turns, variances in speed, and excitement along the way.

Let's say you're about to play a game. In your animated voice, you might want to say something like this:

LET'S HAVE SOME FUN AND PLAY A NEW GAME!

Consistency is the most important ingredient when you're using the voices. For example, if you are trying to tell the children about something fun, it is only natural to use an animated voice. In our workshops, we try to prove this theory by asking adults to say, "Let's have some fun and play a new game," in an unenthusiastic voice that's anything but animated. If they use this Eeyore-like voice to introduce a game, the children will be bored before they even begin. This shows how important it is to connect your voice with the message you're trying to convey. When you use the animated voice, the excitement is contagious and the kids will have a great time, too. You can reflect on your work as an artist by providing what's needed in order to convey the message you want to convey. You can make any situation fun and exciting by using the animated voice.

## Firm and Fair Voice

Use the firm and fair tone of voice as a positive but firm way to communicate directions to children. It's a calm, level voice that receives attention. To correlate your body language with a firm and fair voice, it's important to have a very direct, unfaltering presence with an open posture. Feet are planted on the ground, eye contact is straightforward, and facial expressions are natural.

Imagine a train chugging on a straight, level track—it travels at a steady, even pace. That's the firm and fair voice.

When giving directions at the end of a game, in your firm and fair voice you might say something like this:

# Now   it's time   to put   everything   away.

In our workshops, we ask teachers to try first asking children to put everything away in a playful voice. If they used this voice in the classroom, children would be apt not to take the direction seriously. If you're giving directions in a playful voice, you're being inconsistent. In giving directions, it's important to provide something concrete and matter-of-fact for the children to follow. By pausing on each word, you can provide the consistent message children need in order to respond to the directions you are giving.

## Limit-Setting Voice

The tone of this voice is the opposite of shouting or yelling. Instead of the voice going up, it goes down in a positive way. The limit-setting voice lets you remain calm while setting boundaries. When lowering the tone of your voice, you can get children's attention without making the situation escalate. Often you and the situation can get out of control when you raise the volume and tone of your voice. Your body language should send a consistent, clear, and indisputable message when using the limit-setting voice. For example, your body might take a very strong stance, leaning forward slightly, with feet planted on the floor and a serious facial expression that sets absolute limits. The power struggle with children is eliminated when your voice goes down with a positive reminder that the voice is to have children help themselves to correct their behavior. The limit-setting voice is like the escalator that takes you downstairs—an evenly descending ride that travels at a calm, consistent pace.

Let's say children start fooling around after playing a game, instead of following your directions to clean up. With your limit-setting voice, you might say something like:

STOP FOOLING AROUND. PLEASE PICK UP THE TOYS NOW.

When we introduce the limit-setting voice, we first ask adults to try saying something with their voices going up. When your voice goes up, it may sound as if you are asking a question instead of setting a limit. By using the limit-setting voice, you see how much stronger it is to say, "Stop fooling around. Please pick up the toys now," in a voice that goes down and allows no room for a question to be asked. If you use the animated voice in this situation, you encourage the child to continue the energy that you want to stop. Although the firm and fair voice is appropriate for giving directions, it doesn't convey the proper message to stop what's happening. The limit-setting voice puts things to a halt and provides you with the time to regroup and take charge of the situation with renewed energy.

You can use the voices throughout your day to convey the message you want to get across—and not just when you're speaking to kids. You can use them when making a presentation, speaking at a parent-teacher meeting, or negotiating the price of a new car. Now you have the tools to have fun with your voice and body language and to compose a kind of one-person symphony. Feel free to mix and match the voices when appropriate.

When working with kids, if you speak in an animated voice all the time, you might overexcite them. If you speak in the firm and fair voice constantly, children probably won't get excited and will treat everything as if it were ordinary. If you use the limit-setting voice all of the time, you might block creativity. Using each voice in its proper context allows children to be themselves in every aspect of their lives. And using a voice that does not match the situation can give children a mixed message and lead to inconsistency and confusion before you can even teach them the skills.

One way to reflect on whether you're being consistent with your voice and body language is to imagine that you are being videotaped. Would your voice and body language look and sound as if they match the message you want to convey? Remember, too, that the voices are natural, not rigid. They're not meant to take away our individuality or personality. They are examples to help guide us when communicating with children.

So when asking a child to set the table or do chores, you might want to use your firm and fair voice. At the dinner table, after an exciting day, perhaps you want to use your animated voice in sharing stories about your day and in asking a child to tell you about his day. However, if a child is acting silly at the dinner table, you might find your limit-setting voice to be most effective. When she stops acting inappropriately, go back to that animated voice and tell her what a great job she's done and that she should be proud of herself. It's important to go back and be positive and use the animated voice in order to respond to the change that your child has made happen. These are only suggestions. Every situation is unique, and your use of the voices and body language may vary. You know your child best, and you know the appropriate voice and body language to use. Don't be afraid to break old habits, but remember to be natural and have fun mixing and matching the voices.

## Providing Structure

Structure is crucial to everyone's development. The Mississippi River is broad, bold, and powerful when it runs its course down to the sea; when it overflows its banks, it is destructive, uncontrolled, and lethal. A fire in the hearth on a cold winter's night is beautiful and soothing, warming to the body and the soul. A fire that breaks out of the hearth can destroy a home.

The same is true with humans. Children are bundles of energy and enthusiasm, eager to soak up the world around them and learn everything they can. But if they have no structure, they cannot learn efficiently, they can't cooperate with others, they can't grow into the full adults that they have the right to become.

When we are working or living with children, it is important to provide them with a consistent structure. Children want and need structure because it provides a safe environment. It's our job as adults to impart it by establishing a consistent bottom line. A bottom line is a combination of rules, limits, and expectations.

All children test their boundaries with adults. One child might go to one adult to get what he wants, and if he doesn't get his way he might go to the other adult. It's important that adults give children the same consistent message so that children know what's expected of them. When children test limits, we can use the limit-setting voice and set a bottom line. For example, if a child is acting out, we can be firm and help her redirect her behavior from the very beginning. When children get away with small things, they continue to push their boundaries farther and farther. In the classroom, kids might constantly call out. At home, they might always become noisy and disruptive before bedtime. If you don't notice these things and set a limit the first time, the boundaries of your structure begin to fall apart. This inconsistency in your bottom line can confuse children and not give them the structure they need, causing them to establish inappropriate patterns of power and control.

When setting a limit, it is important to remain calm and use the proper voice and body language to convey a message that resolves the situation in a positive way. Sometimes I have a hard time setting limits when it's time for my son to go to bed. I can be too playful. If you ask kids in an animated way to go to bed, they are more likely to fool around than take you seriously. Rather than bickering with them, simply state in your limit-setting voice, "Please get ready for bed now." When limit-setting, it's important to be concise. The fewer words you use, the clearer and more direct your message. When you use fewer words, children don't have the chance to test your limits or get the attention they would with more words.

In a classroom, if kids are calling out, stop what you are doing and use your limit-setting voice to explain that they must raise their hands if they want to speak, so that we can all learn. If you let just one child call out and don't nip this behavior in the bud, things start to unravel. It is difficult to go back and establish a consistent structure—and you spend a lot of time in tugs-of-war with your kids. Once a child is following your directions, it is important to let her know that she is doing a great job and should be proud of herself.

Children need to understand that when they are not listening to the rules, limits, or expectations, you will take charge and help them to regain their self-control for themselves. Structure provides a climate of safety and well-being for all of us. A roller coaster can be great fun, but imagine the same ride without the boundaries of seat belts, roll bars, or other safety precautions. The absence of structure can turn the same joyful ride into a dangerous adventure.

It is important for kids to understand that adults also need to stay within the boundaries and follow directions. You can explain that when adults don't abide by the law and follow the speed limit, they can get speeding tickets or possibly injure someone. In places like New York City's Times Square, the so-called broken-windows strategy of policing, in which authorities stopped tolerating minor acts of vandalism, graffiti, and rowdiness, is credited with cutting down such major crimes as murder and armed robbery. If people are presented with guidelines that are applied fairly and consistently, they tend to be more apt to follow them because they know what's expected of them from the start.

In his book *Between Teacher and Child*, Haim Ginott wrote, "I have become aware of a personal paradox: I often use tactics similar to those I try to eradicate in my pupils. I raise my voice to end noise. I use force to break up fighting. I am rude to a child who is impolite, and I berate a child who uses bad language." This proves the adage that we should practice what we preach. It is up to us, as adults, not to "dance to children's tunes" but to create our own music on our own terms. Providing a consistent structure and bottom line helps us do just that.

## Letting Go

Often we try to protect kids from reality. However, in some cases we need to provide them skills to deal with real-life situations. In

E. B. White's *Charlotte's Web*, the spider very delicately tells Wilbur about the reality of her impending death. But her wonderful gift to Wilbur is helping him to develop skills to succeed once she is gone. It's our duty to give our children skills so we *can* let go and help them become independent.

Andrew Stanton, the director of the movie *Finding Nemo*, told *Disney Magazine* how he got the idea for the movie when walking with his son. "I spent the entire walk talking to my son to stay away from the curb, to watch for cars, not to touch things. I was so overprotective. That got me thinking about the premise that fear can keep a good father from being one. I think the story idea that was quickly settled on was the nobility of a parent trying to do everything to look out for his child but being able to let go."

While I was in high school, my best friend, Roger DeAngelis, and I decided to make a theatrical film; we were thirty years ahead of Matt Damon and Ben Affleck. The film had two male leads and a heroine.

It didn't take us long to cast the male leads, but finding the right teenage female took longer—we were at an all-boys school, after all. One afternoon, when I was at home, the phone rang. I picked up and heard a breathlessly excited Roger announcing, "I've got the heroine." Unfortunately, I didn't hear my mother picking up the extension. Within minutes, she and my father were in my room, confronting me.

"We know about your drug use," she said, "and we know that Roger is your dealer."

They were chagrined when I explained that this kind of heroine ended in an "e" and wasn't snorted or injected. They slunk away and never brought up the subject again—and they never listened in on any more of my phone conversations. While my mother had little contact with us, as you can see, she was an egregious phone snoop. Though she loved me, she invested too much energy in control and not enough in promoting my independence.

The point of this story is that all of us must learn the importance of letting go. Whether we are raising children, or dealing with spouses or partners or coworkers, we must not just help them but also help them to help themselves. It is up to us to help children control themselves and, therefore, take ownership.

We can give children positive reinforcement by first asking them whom they should be proud of (themselves), or telling them what a great job they've done by saying that they should be proud of themselves. This helps children feel the ownership of their actions. Of course, after that, it's natural to share with your children that *you're* proud of them too.

As our children grow, they must develop this skill. As grown-ups, we cannot always depend on others to tell us what a good job we've done. We need to tell ourselves that. Children must learn this at an early age. With the busy schedules that children balance among school, after-school activities, extracurricular activities, and their home lives, the reality is that there may not always be an adult around to tell them he or she is proud of them. And if children have this expectation, they will be disappointed. That's why it's important to let go and let children feel the pride within themselves.

It's important to remind kids that it is up to them to manage their own actions. We hear teachers say, "Do your homework for me." Parents say, "Do me a favor and clean up your room." When we give these sorts of instructions to kids, we are telling them that they should do things for us. But for whom should the kids really be doing these things? Not for the adult, but for themselves.

When we change our language to give ownership of their lives to the children, we remind them that they are in control of their own behavior. Teachers can say, "For your science homework, read this chapter so that you can be prepared for tomorrow's experiment. You're not doing your homework for me, you're doing it for yourself." And parents can say, "Please clean up your room so that the dust doesn't make you sneeze and so you can find your guitar pick; remember, you're not doing it for me, you're doing it for yourself." This way, we can let children know that it's up to them to follow directions because they are the people in charge of helping themselves.

Recently I had a hard time letting go and admitting to myself that my son is getting older and more independent. Some of my son's friends invited him to go to a dance at their school. It was Andy's first dance, and I was more nervous than he was. After he left, I couldn't stop thinking about him: hoping that he was having a good time and getting along with all of the new kids he was meeting there. My wife kept reminding me that I needed to let go and that Andy was fine—I was the one who was having a hard time. When we returned from dinner, there was a message from Andy on the answering machine, telling us that we had forgotten to give him money to buy refreshments.

As we drove over to the dance, I started wondering if I had "forgotten" to give him the money with some subliminal purpose. By bringing the money over to him, I was giving myself the opportunity to check in on him and see how he was doing. Andy met me at the door; he was having a great time. As I got back into the car, I put my arm around the seat and said to my wife, "Everything's going to be fine." And the person sitting next

to me turned to me and said, "Sure it is, but you're not my type."
I had been so nervous about Andy that I had climbed into the
wrong car and had put my arm around a man I'd never met. I'm
still learning to let go so I can help give Andy the skills he needs
and trust that he has the skills to handle any situation that arises.

# How to Use This Book

## Sequencing the Skills

The upcoming chapters are in a sequence that mirrors the
way we teach the ABCs of Life, beginning with the Pledge for
Success, then presenting the skills of Self-Control, Self-Control
Time, Self-Confidence, Responsibility and Consequences, Thinking and Problem Solving, and Cooperation.

The Pledge for Success first lays the foundation for the skills
and is an important ingredient in the process that helps both
children and adults to take ownership of the ABCs of Life. Then
we discuss each skill in turn, in a chapter of its own, with both a
narrative to explain the importance of the skill and a practical
section to help you teach and use each skill. The order of the
skills is not arbitrary—it's a time-tested sequence. It is important
to introduce the skills sequentially because each skill builds on
the one before. Just as you can't teach a child to write a sentence
before he or she can form the letters of the alphabet, you can't
teach responsibility before you teach self-control. The program
is not about memorizing the definition or rote learning, it's
about using the skill in everyday life. Use your best judgment to
look for evidence of understanding and internalization to deter-
mine when to move on to the next skill in the sequence.

When I was getting my master's degree at Lesley University,

# THE ABCs OF LIFE
# SEQUENCING THE SKILLS

* **Pledge for Success:** The Pledge is a promise that children make to themselves, with an emphasis on respect, listening, diversity, and trying their best. It builds a foundation for all of the skills.

* **Self-Control:** After learning the Pledge for Success, children can then learn to use their self-control to control what they do and what they say.

* **Self-Control Time:** In order to calm down, relax, and get their self-control back, children take Self-Control Time.

* **Self-Confidence:** When children use their self-control and try their best, they give themselves the proud, happy feeling called self-confidence.

* **Responsibility and Consequences:** With self-control and self-confidence, children can take responsibility for themselves and understand the consequences of their actions.

* **Thinking and Problem Solving:** When children take responsibility and realize the consequences of their actions, they can think for themselves and problem-solve.

* **Cooperation:** When children use their self-control, have self-confidence, take responsibility, and use their thinking and problem-solving abilities, they can cooperate with others.

For your convenience, you'll find a copy of the above guide in the Appendix. You can cut it out and use it as needed.

I created lessons and activities for practical use in the classroom. My teachers always asked me to back them up with education-ally sound research. I realized that the theories of the great psy-chologists Jean Piaget and Abraham Maslow were crucial to developing many of those lessons. Piaget helped shape our un-derstanding of how children learn. He pointed out that children go through sequential stages of development. For example, a baby first begins to crawl, then uses that knowledge of motion to learn how to walk. One skill naturally builds on the next. I was excited to think of the practical applications of this theory: We make sounds before we can talk; we learn the alphabet before we can read; we use training wheels before we can ride a two-wheeler. I used Piaget's insights then and continued to use them in the years it took to develop the program.

Abraham Maslow pointed out that humans have a variety of needs. These needs, he pointed out, have different priorities. For example, we must satisfy our bodily needs, like hunger and thirst, before satisfying our needs for companionship and be-longing.

Just as Piaget and Maslow's skills build on each other, the ABCs of Life work sequentially: The Pledge for Success creates a foundation that all of the other skills build on. For instance, a child must learn how to use self-control before learning to cooperate with others. Additionally, the skills of Lesson One satisfy a person's basic need for success in life—if people do not have the skills, then they are not able to make their lives their own.

Whether this is used at home, in the classroom, or in the community, we don't simply teach one skill, then move on to the next. Each day, we recapitulate the skills we have already talked about, making sure that kids understand and continue to apply them daily. We ask parents, guardians, and teachers to go over the skills with the kids, beginning each day with the Pledge for Success. This doesn't mean that kids internalize skills instantly; in fact, that process occurs over time. Every day, as we play the games, share stories, and discuss the skills, we are helping the kids internalize everything they have learned.

## Teaching the ABCs of Life

As I mentioned, each part of the Pledge for Success and each skill ends with a practical, hands-on approach to teaching the ABCs of Life. In each, you will find an easy-to-follow progression to teach each skill: *Introduce and Define It*, *Experience It*, and *Share It*. This is all you need to get started with the skills. Each section exemplifies the great variety of ways you can approach teaching the skills. It is important to go over all three sections with your child. The ABCs of Life was designed with different learning styles in mind, among them sensory, experiential, and motor. And they are success oriented so that children at any ability or level can achieve.

Rather than telling you what to do, we provide you with the foundation for teaching the ABCs of Life. Have fun introducing and defining each skill so that kids can understand it, experiencing each skill so that they can internalize it, and sharing the skill so that children can apply it to their lives.

## Introduce and Define It

I found out early in my career the importance of defining words we use with kids. Once, I was teaching a lesson that required students to focus. They were having difficulty, so I kept telling them to concentrate—to no avail. I soon realized that the kids had no idea what I was talking about. Finally, I asked, "Does anyone know what 'concentrate' means?"

Hands shot up.

I called on one youngster, who proudly answered, "Orange juice!"

It was an "aha moment" for me. I thought that maybe these kids didn't know what other skills like self-control were either. I later did a survey around the school and found out that one-third of all the students thought concentrate meant orange juice. We've known teachers who have talked about self-confidence in their classroom starting in September, and when we've visited their classroom in May the kids asked us, "What does self-confidence mean?" And this has happened with many of the skills we teach.

How can kids understand any of these types of skills without having someone first define them? Universal definitions give us all the same point of reference. A red light means stop almost anywhere in the world. Imagine if every country or every state had different signals for traffic to stop. Things as simple as right or left could create confusion if we all didn't have the same understanding of what they mean. If we were asking for directions, and in one town right meant left and left meant right, we'd never find our destination. Maps consistently use north, south, east, and west as universally understood coordinates. In boating, the common language of bow and stern is not easily confused. In most countries, we drive on the right side of the road. Visit England and you'll find yourself driving on the left side. Imagine the confusion some people feel when they first drive on the side of the road opposite the one they're used to. Consistency is crucial to defining and teaching the skills of life.

Almost from the beginning of time, humankind has searched

for ways to communicate. First oral language developed, then early forms of written communication sprung up. In the Far East, people used graphic representations of real objects instead of alphabets; modern Chinese and Japanese characters derive from these early drawings. In France, the ancient caves of Lascaux contain drawings that tell stories; Egyptian hieroglyphics were a similarly picture-based form of communication.

It was only when symbols, and then alphabets, came into use—among the Minoans, the Greeks, and other peoples of the Mediterranean and Asia Minor—that humans could achieve universal understanding of each other. You could write a symbol on a piece of papyrus in Linear B, or write letters in Attic Greek or any other language—and send it miles away to someone else who would be able to understand what you had in mind without even having to see you in person. These forms of communication helped make their culture universal. We're trying to achieve something similar in our culture—a common set of references and skills that everybody understands.

In Europe, so many different currencies existed that, in 1999, most countries adopted the euro, in part to avoid the difficulty of changing money again and again, even on a one-day drive. In American law, so many business regulations varied from state to state that Congress had to pass the Uniform Commercial Code, just so that what was legal for a company to do in one state wouldn't be illegal in another. That's why we have to use consistent language to define skills to children; they have to be on exactly the same page that we are on. If we all had the same vocabulary and the same skills, imagine the impact it would have on schools, communities, and the culture as a whole.

As a practical approach to defining the ABCs of Life, we include easy-to-use posters of the Pledge for Success and the skills in the Appendix. Cut out the poster and read and discuss the definitions with your child. Then you can place it somewhere prominent in your house, perhaps on a refrigerator or bulletin board, and refer to it throughout the day. That way, you can establish a consistent language and get ready to do games and activities that will help children experience the skills.

## Experience It

As you'll read in the coming chapters, we designed our learning games and activities to be fun for people of all ages; we use a "play vocabulary" that everyone can understand—Slinky and Etch-A-Sketch, Pick-Up Sticks, and bubbles. The games and activities use classic toys that can amuse adults as much as they enthrall children. They also speak to the theories of the early educational pioneer John Dewey. His discoveries that children learn by doing had a large influence on the development of Lesson One. As you will see, games as simple as blowing bubbles and telling kids to use their self-control not to break them can have a huge impact on children. They are experiencing self-control, understanding it, and internalizing it—and they will be able to make use of it throughout their lives.

In developing the experiential components of the ABCs of Life, I tried never to lose sight of the idea of universality; if something worked for kids, it had to work for adults too. I once met Mel Stuart, the director of *Willy Wonka and the Chocolate Factory*. He shared with me that he created the movie with adults in mind. I think that is the secret to the success of so many books, movies, and theme parks and is also one of the reasons the Lesson One program has been successful: The activities appeal to that childlike quality in adults and kids alike.

Within the chapters of this book, we introduce you to the

games and activities and help you understand how they help your children internalize the skills. It is important that you internalize the skills for yourself before introducing them to a child. When playing these games, it's important to have fun but to not get overly silly. We should treat the teaching of skills such as self-control and responsibility as we teach kids reading, writing, or even tying their shoes. The presentation should be light-hearted and engaging, but not ridiculous. For example, in many of the movement games, we suggest that you vary your speed as you lead the game. However, if you go impossibly fast or absurdly slow, the children may see that as an opportunity to take the game and the skill less seriously. It's also important to remember that no one is ever "out." Rather, these games are geared so that every child is included, feeling a sense of accomplishment and success. A game like musical chairs, although it can be fun, excludes children from playing. We don't want children to feel excluded or embarrassed because they can't play the game. We want children to experience the success of trying their best or using their self-control.

Most Americans have heard of Coney Island, even if they've never been there. For decades, the little spit of land out at the south end of Brooklyn, the terminus of a number of subway lines, has been synonymous with fun and good times. The beach and the boardwalk, the amusement parks, the legendary rides like the Cyclone, long the most fearsome roller coaster in America; the parachute drop, and the Panama Slide, which to a young child seemed a thousand stories high and provided an unforgettable sense of excitement when, sitting on a sisal mat, he pushed off down the sleek mahogany surface for the breathtaking streak down into the well at the bottom—these were the stuff that children's dreams were made of.

Effie took us there; she loved the place, and so did we. (Could it be that her love of amusement parks came from the fact that she shared a birthday with Walt Disney? Probably not, but she had the same childlike love of fun and wonder.) When I saw her eyes sparkle with delight at the rides and the attractions, the caramel corn and the carnival glitter, I was happy. Then I looked around and saw something I hadn't realized: On the rides, in the water, at the booths, were people of all ages. Adults and the kids they brought with them were enjoying the fun equally.

This was my first glimmer of an insight that would become crucial to Lesson One: We are all human, no matter what our age. Adults and kids have universal interests. Everything about us—our likes, our needs, our obligations—doesn't somehow change when we reach the age of twenty-one. When Wordsworth wrote, in "Intimations of Immortality," "The child is father to the man," he was summing up the same idea. The adult still holds within the wonder and enthusiasm of the child he or she once was. In my many trips to the Disney theme parks, I have constantly taken notice of people of all ages and cultures enjoying the rides and attractions as they experience them together. Among the feelings are joy on the merry-go-round, fear in the haunted house, adventure on the Peter Pan ride, and nervous anticipation on Space Mountain, and, in the free-falling elevator car in the Tower of Terror, you feel . . . well, let's just say that ride is aptly named. No matter what age we are, we all experience similar feelings.

"We're sure of just one thing," Walt Disney once said. "Everybody in the world was once a child. We grow up, our personalities change, but in every one of us something remains of our childhood. All of us are simple and naive without prejudice and bias. We're friendly and trusting. It just seems to me that if your picture hits that spot in one person, it's going to hit that same spot in almost everybody. So, in planning a new picture, we don't think of grown-ups, we don't think of children, but just of that fine, clean, unspoiled spot down deep in every one of us that maybe the world has made us forget and that maybe our pictures can help recall."

Both you and your child will experience what each skill means in an enjoyable way in the "Experience It" section that appears after each skill chapter. We provide a practical explanation of each game or activity that accompanies a skill. And then you can go back to the definition of the skill and connect it to the experience that you had playing the game.

## Share It

In ancient Greece, the word was *aoidos;* in modern Africa, it's *griot;* in America we say *storyteller.* The tradition is as old as humanity, and as valuable. For many millennia, people have gone from village to village, town to town, city to city, even nowadays on radio and television, to share stories. Some are true, some are fictional, many are combinations of both; their purpose has always been to recount the human experience and to give others the benefit of the storyteller's insight. It's a tradition Lesson One has tried to keep alive.

To help children apply the skills to their everyday lives, we need to naturally share stories from our lives and encourage children to share their stories too. We are all natural storytellers. Take Bill Cosby, for example. He doesn't just tell jokes, he tells stories that talk about the human condition. These stories have a universal appeal with which we all naturally identify. Your stories have the same appeal. Just like Cosby's, your stories come from the heart and from real-life situations. As you sit down with your children at the dinner table or in the car or, if you're a teacher, in the classroom, make yourself a role model for sharing.

If you ask a child every day how his day was, he may be hesitant to talk; he might feel put on the spot, afraid he might be judged or labeled, or afraid that no one else feels the same way. So first confide in him about your day—the excitement, the frustration, and any other feelings you had; relate the events that you saw and experienced.

When you sketch out the dimensions of your day, children begin to open up and tell you their feelings and experiences from their days—and they don't feel put on the spot. You can tell them about times you have and haven't followed the Pledge for Success and used the skills. If you share a time when you haven't utilized these things, be sure to share what you'd do the next time. This way, you show that you are able to learn from your experiences, and kids will understand that they can learn from their experiences too. When you put yourself in their shoes, they see that we are all going through similar experiences. And at the same time, adults get to share their lives and open up intimacy between themselves and their children. It's up to you to be the catalyst.

As you discuss each skill, remember that kids need to understand the "whys." We need to explain everything we do—from the simplest to the most complex parts of our lives. We say "Thank you" to the tollbooth clerk because that's the way we would like to be treated as well. We learn math because it helps us to learn to think; it also helps us get through life. Counting change, measuring construction projects, calculating distances on maps—all of these require some math skills. We don't study just to get the right answer. Nor do we learn the skills just to get approval from others.

In Louis Sachar's Newbery Award–winning book, *Holes*—which became a much-acclaimed film—the main characters are sent to a detention camp for boys. At the camp, the boys are responsible for only one task: They must dig one hole per day, and the hole must be five feet deep and five feet wide. When the boys ask why they are doing it, they're told that "digging holes builds character," but nothing else. Because they don't know why they're digging these holes, the boys can't learn from what they're doing.

By explaining the reasons why we do things, we help children connect the skills of life on a larger scale. For example, after reading this book and internalizing the skills, you can explain to your child that when she looks out for cars before running into the street to catch a ball, she is actually using her self-control. Now she understands the "why" behind the importance of self-control: It can save lives. The ABCs of Life connect to every aspect of life: When introducing themselves to new friends, kids use the skill of self-confidence; when they do their homework, they are taking responsibility for themselves; when they are working on a science project, they are using their thinking and problem-solving skills; when they are playing in a band, they are cooperating.

Many teachers have told us that, when they tell their stories to kids and have kids tell stories back, the experience not only invigorates individual students but also brings life back into the classroom and into their own lives. One family spoke about their son, who had a rough first few weeks at a new school. He was in a special education class that was isolated from all the other classes, and everything that could go wrong did. One day his teacher brought him down to gym class late. The gym teacher yelled at him in front of everyone. Already feeling isolated, he became angry and embarrassed. Later, when the gym teacher realized that it wasn't the boy's fault that he was late, the gym teacher apologized.

When the parents talked to the teacher about this experience and others, the teacher admitted that she felt bad for the experiences their son had been having. She told them that when she was a kid she also had a tough time in junior high, and she said she became a teacher because she wanted kids to have a positive experience in school. But she didn't know what to do to help him. The parents suggested that the teacher tell their son about her experiences in school and the reason why she became a teacher. They hoped that would help him understand that she was trying her best and that, perhaps, they could work together to create a positive experience for him. It worked like a charm. The boy's eyes lit up, and he began to confide in his teacher for the first time.

The conventional wisdom about the TV show *Seinfeld* is that it is a show about "nothing." But really, it is not about nothing; it's about the small events that happen in everyday life. The reason for the show's popularity is that we all identify with the everyday moments in life. Using stories from real-life situations has a long tradition. Carl Reiner was one of the first situation-comedy writers to survey his staff about funny and interesting things that occurred in their daily lives and include those stories in *The Dick Van Dyke Show* plotlines. Other shows like *The Cosby Show* and *Everbody Loves Raymond* have followed suit with that same philosophy.

With our hectic schedules, we often don't take time for conversations about daily events in our lives. At home, we tend to be busy with errands and chores; children often immediately turn to video games and television when they have downtime. The same thing happens to adults. At work, they may spend the bulk of their days interacting with computer keys and screens. They might come home to spend their time unwinding by watching television or typing away in an Internet chat room.

The telling of stories is becoming a lost art. In today's culture, it's something that we don't often do. It's natural to take time to share what we did last weekend or last night with our coworkers, friends, or families. We can also share stories with children. Kids love hearing about the lives of the adults around them. They can learn from stories that you tell as much as they can from facts. Adding stories to the relationship creates a new dimension in the way that you look at each other.

We're eager to talk about our lives—and I see the same eagerness in children's eyes as they tell me about times when they used their self-control or any other skill. Our infatuation with reality television and made-for-television biographies should show us one thing: Everyone's life could make a compelling biography. We all have important stories to tell. Sharing everyday moments at home and school brings back intimacy to our lives.

Once the skills are defined, experienced, and shared, talk to kids about how they connect to everyday life. The ABCs of Life can be found everywhere: on television, in books, in activities. When you read a book or watch television, discuss with kids which characters are using what skills and how they are using them. Discuss how the ones who aren't using the skills could have. Would this change the outcome of the story? When you're doing an activity with your child, talk about the skills. If you're playing checkers, you can tell your child to think of the wide variety of possibilities for moves she could make, just as she thinks of the variety of ways to approach a school essay. You can talk about the skills in everyday life: as children are taking a test at school (it takes self-control not to look at someone else's paper), deciding what snack they want to eat (this takes thinking), trying a new activity (this takes self-confidence), doing their chores (this takes responsibility), or going to play with a friend (in this situation, it's important to treat others the way we want to be treated).

Talk to kids about people in your life who use these skills in their daily lives. After learning about each skill, discuss with your child a role model you had who has this skill, then ask your child to discuss a role model of his who has this skill. Just as stories have been passed down through generations, wonderful skills can be passed down from generation to generation. Important people in your life can be role models for you. Even though some are gone, you can still emulate their use of the skills. Some lyrics of the song "You'll Be in My Heart" from the Disney movie *Tarzan* say what I feel:

> . . . *you'll be in my heart*
> *From this day on, now and forever more*

Passing along skills is a way to keep role models alive in the hearts of children and adults.

How do we continue to make personal connections in a world of modern technology? Our information age is a wondrous thing. We can communicate with people all over the world using the Internet. It's exciting to share stories, ask questions, and relate to others in ways that are easier over the Internet. It has become a new way to meet and fall in love; many marriages have started in front of two flickering screens of pixels. It has even saved lives. One woman, virtually paralyzed with back pain, was unable to get to a phone and able only to reach her son's computer to ask for help. Online strangers came to her rescue and called 911.

Still, if our only social contact is through chat rooms with people we don't know, we sacrifice the uniqueness of face-to-face conversations, we lose a special kind of intimacy in our own lives. Lack of intimacy and communication ruptures our culture and leads to feelings of alienation, isolation, and, in its worst form, violence. Relating life stories and lessons to the skills makes these stories into teachable moments between adult and child. It's the missing link in many of our lives.

On all of my travels around the country, both adults and kids have told me amazing stories; they relate to all of us. No matter who we are, we all can learn from how others use Lesson One. I've included some of these stories in the "Share It" sections of this book. After sharing and reflecting on these narratives with your child, you can tell stories of your own to bring the skills to life. We've also designed discussion starters to look at the entire spectrum of each skill area. These can serve as a jumping-off point for your discussions. The excitement surrounding the skills resides within your stories and discussions.

Just as there is no such thing as making a perfect golf swing every time you try, there is no such thing as mastering the ABCs of Life. You can have an excellent golf technique, but that doesn't mean that you always hit a perfect shot. And even if we have internalized the ABCs of Life, we still strive to incorporate them into our lives. Even though I developed *Lesson One: The ABCs of Life*, I need this book just as much as anyone else. I constantly need to go back and define the skills, ensure that my voice is consistent, and remind myself to share the "whys." Learning the ABCs of Life is a process, just as life is a process. We are all human and we are going to make mistakes. So on occasions when your voice goes up or if you are not consistent with your limits, take the time to look back at the essentials. The important

# THE ESSENTIALS FOR TEACHING THE ABCs OF LIFE

* Use positive language.

* Let go and put ownership back on your child.

* Teach the skills sequentially.

* Use varied voices in a manner consistent with your message: firm and fair, animated, and limit-setting voices.

* Provide a consistent structure with a firm "bottom line."

* Define the skills.

* Share the "whys."

* Play the games to experience the skills.

* Share the stories from yourself; then have your child share.

* Use the discussion starters to take the skills to a new level of understanding.

For your convenience, you'll find a copy of the above guide in the Appendix. You can cut it out and use it as needed.

thing is to be yourself and to take ownership of the skills, learn from mistakes, and keep trying. The ABCs of Life can help us all as we navigate our way through life.

Turn the page and step into the world of Lesson One. It will change the lives of the children around you. It will change your life too.

# 4

# The Pledge for Success

Like a poorly dubbed foreign film, my life often seemed one beat out of step; it didn't match the culture around me. As a kid, I always felt different because my family wasn't like anyone else's. Then, over time, I saw families change. The culture seemed to catch up with many of my life experiences. Male and female roles slowly changed for the better, with women not having to stay at home unless they chose to. But that positive change left many families in our society with a dilemma: Who should care for the children? Over time, divorce rates and single-parent homes gradually became more commonplace, providing a new definition of family. In addition, in an ever-changing economy, many people had to work longer and harder. Often, a child was the last person to leave home and the first to return; even young children found themselves required to take care of their baby brothers and sisters. I identified with these new family models—after all, my parents were never around.

As technology increased, there seemed to be an ever-growing lack of communication within families. Kids and adults began to turn to computers, video games, television, videos, and DVDs to take the place of family time; that, too, took a toll on adult-child relations. Technology, while exciting, has contributed to a lack of communicating, listening, and sharing among families. I could easily empathize with kids who grew up without ever connecting with their parents. Still, I saw children comparing themselves to their friends and thinking that something was wrong with their families. I wanted them to be able to see that there are many different kinds of families and one is not any better than another.

During my childhood with Effie, we encountered a lot of prejudice together, especially about the issue of family. Because she was African American, people assumed she was our maid or babysitter, and in some cases, they treated her as if she were beneath them. As a young child, I didn't understand why other people didn't recognize Effie for who she was to me: my mom. One Christmas Eve, Effie put an African American Santa Claus in her window. Although I never thought of people in terms of color, it had never occurred to me that Santa Claus could be anything but white. I then realized that Santa didn't always have to be white, and it bothered me that the world around me didn't accept the possibility that there was more than one way to look at things. Why couldn't Santa Claus be any color?

Since I had such an early exposure to diversity through Effie, I even asked my elementary school teacher why the people illustrated in our schoolbooks were all white. I wanted an opportunity to explain what my life was really like. She dismissed my question as silly. I was hurt and angry because I wasn't being listened to and my life experience was being negated. All of these images had an indelible effect on me. Over time, I realized that I was not alone. The unwillingness of many people to treat others well was escalating in our culture. My experiences have made treating others well and celebrating the diversity of families, cultures, interests, and even learning styles a very important part in teaching the ABCs of Life.

I didn't choose the circumstances that I was given; no one does. All we can do is try our best, no matter what the circumstance. I realized that most people simply wanted to be able to try their best, but the culture often told them that their best wasn't good enough, that winning the game and getting the best grade were more important than the process of living life and learning from the mistakes we make every day. All around me, I saw many people living in a similar pressure cooker. Something had to be done.

I wanted a way to translate my own experiences into something that would help kids and adults to have a road map to guide them through life, and the Pledge for Success is just that. The Pledge for Success is a promise that children make to themselves, with an emphasis on trying their best, respect, listening, and diversity. It builds a foundation for all of the skills. Of course, we will continue to make mistakes, not listen on occasion, and not treat others as we'd like to be treated all the time, but we can at least have a point of reference that helps us to set a goal we can strive for. Through personal and professional experiences, we at Lesson One developed the Pledge for Success along with teachers, parents, and school administrators throughout the nation, who explained their visions of what children—and our entire society—needed.

Adults and children need more than just facts and figures to make their way through society and culture, yet we often assume that they somehow pick up these skills as they go through life. As you've seen from some of the stories we've told already, that isn't always true. Not every home is a traditional one; not all adults have the skills themselves, let alone the ability to pass them on.

When you walk into an elementary school classroom in America, you inevitably see the alphabet and number lines on the wall. At home and at school we refer to these basics whenever we are helping a child learn to read or to perform math equations. These are important for living in our society, of course. But why isn't life itself also a school subject? The Pledge for Success helps make it one: It equips children with the foundation that helps them to be successful in life. Like the skills, it is as basic as the alphabet or the numerals, and can easily become as integral a tool at home and school.

When we talk about the Pledge for Success, we talk about how it works for both adults and kids. The Pledge provides a structure on which you can build a successful life. The structure provides a safe environment—and if kids are in a safe place, they have the chance to grow and succeed.

If you are an adult, you can provide the structure and consistency a child needs. Remember, the Pledge is not a set of values or a spiritual document. Values and spirituality are intensely private issues that each of us must decide on individually. The Pledge for Success is based on a set of universal skills that all humans—in any country, in any culture, at any age—must learn for a successful life. Most important, the Pledge is a promise that every child or adult makes to himself or herself. When we keep the Pledge, we are keeping our word to ourselves; when we break it, we are letting only ourselves down.

We are always careful to make sure that kids understand that they are the true owners of the Pledge. It is not meant to be formulaic or to be recited by rote. For that reason, we add a "why" for each part of the Pledge, so that children do not just read and recite it but actually understand and internalize the Pledge.

Both adults and children make a promise to themselves to apply the Pledge for Success in their day-to-day lives. It is not a set of rules forced on us by others. We make a promise to ourselves ultimately so that we can be proud of ourselves. If we don't keep that promise, we don't feel proud of ourselves. We can help children understand this concept by asking them for whom they are following the Pledge—remind them that they are doing it for themselves. We can also provide them with positive reminders that they should be proud of themselves when they follow the Pledge. Very quickly, kids learn to make the Pledge for Success an essential part of their lives.

The Pledge for Success is necessary for children and adults to live happy, successful, and productive lives. It was designed to help kids and adults learn to deal with some common problems in our culture. It took a whole lifetime to develop the Pledge for Success. In the story of *Peter Pan*, we discover the magical world of Never-Never Land, where people can be children forever; this doesn't happen in real life. However, the Pledge provides adults and children with a ticket to Never-Never Land. It provides a structure of safety and trust that lets us keep our childlike qualities, while at the same time helping us with the skills to grow up and deal with the realities of our everyday lives.

# I Will Listen to What Others Have to Say

A friend of mine recently had a problem with his cell phone. He called the phone company and, after ten minutes or so on hold, finally got through to a human.

LESSON ONE

# Pledge for Success

## A Promise I Make to Myself

### I will listen to what others have to say.

When I wait my turn to speak, I can hear what everyone has to say.

### I will treat others the way I would like to be treated.

Pushing, fighting, bullying, name-calling, and treating others badly hurts them and hurts me.

### I will respect the diversity of all people.

Whether we are the same or different on the outside, it's the person we are on the inside that counts.

### I will remember that I have people who care about me in my family, school, and community.

Families, like schools and communities, can be many sizes and made up of all kinds of people.

### I will try my best.

Even when I make mistakes, I learn from them. The most important thing is to keep trying.

"I can't turn my cell phone on," he explained. "I pushed the On button and the display didn't light up. I tried using two different chargers, but the phone wouldn't work."

"Are you calling from the phone now?" the agent asked.

"I can't turn it on," he replied.

"What happens when you turn it on?"

"I can't turn it on."

"What does the display say?"

"I can't get the display on."

"Have you tried charging it?"

"I've tried two different chargers."

"Have you tried more than one charger?"

It didn't take long for my friend to realize that the agent wasn't listening to a word he said. She had been trained to ask a series of questions, and she was going to ask them, even though the answers to all her questions were contained in the few words he had spoken as soon as they were connected. Her superiors didn't teach her the importance of listening to her customers and providing a good customer-service experience; rather, their goals were focused on following procedures.

As a society, we often talk past each other. Parents and children, husbands and wives, teachers and students—we frequently fail to actually hear what the other person is saying. Television and radio shock-talk shows have done a lot to encourage this trend; hosts actively bait their guests, inducing them to shout at each other until nobody is listening.

The results of this kind of a culture can be devastating. A physician who failed to listen to his assistants, or read the clinical notes, operated on the wrong side of a woman's brain. The pilots of Korean Airlines flight 007, shot down by the old Soviet Union, apparently misheard the directions for entering coordinates into their autopilot. When we don't listen, we lose the chance to find out what other people have to tell us—even if what they're saying could be very valuable to us.

Sometimes, we expect children to listen to our directions without even knowing what listening is or giving them a chance to practice it. In order to teach kids about the importance of listening, we play a game for both adults and kids called Listen Up.

You can play with one child or with a large group of children. Simply introduce a small list of items within a category, building up to a larger list. Ask the child to repeat the list to you. Talk about how the listening skill she uses when she plays the game is the same skill she uses to listen and follow directions at home and at school. (In each chapter, there are general descriptions like this one that will help give you an overview of the games we play. Practical instructions for all games are also included in the "Experience It" part of the Teaching the ABCs of Life section of each chapter.)

Since this is the first area of the Pledge for Success, listening will help you establish your structure, limits, and boundaries. The Pledge does not give children the freedom to do whatever they want, but it provides the structure kids need to follow directions the first time. Listening and following directions are important for all aspects of the ABCs of Life and sets the tone for the remaining skills.

Discuss how adults have to use their listening too. When adults listen to kids, it gives the adults valuable clues to what's going on in children's lives. They may be excited about a class, or a sport, or a new friend. If you don't listen to kids, you may be communicating the message that you don't care.

Once, I was driving from Boston to New York with Andy, who was then four years old. Although we had a brand-new car, it got a flat tire, and I couldn't figure out how to change it. I called AAA.

When the tow-truck driver arrived, he told me that I needed to find the lug wrench—the tool that came with the car that was specially fitted to that particular wheel's lug nuts. While he was explaining this, Andy kept trying to get my attention. "Dad, Dad," he said repeatedly, and I shushed him. I was listening to the AAA guy and trying to figure out where the lug wrench might be. "Dad, Dad," Andy said again. Again I started to shush him.

"You should listen to your son," the driver told me. I turned around, and there was Andy, holding the lug wrench in his hand. For just one moment, I had forgotten to apply my own lessons: that we should listen to kids, and that kids have skills that we sometimes don't recognize. Although the skills of Lesson One are commonsense, to use them consistently is an exciting challenge. We need to try our best every day in order to internalize these skills and make them into an integral part of our daily lives.

## Teaching the ABCs of Life:
### Listening to Others

· · · · · · · · · · · · · · · · · · · · · · · · · · · · · · · · · · · · · · · · · · · · · · · · · · · · · · · · · · · · · · · · · · · · · · · · · · · · · · · · ·

### 1: INTRODUCE AND DEFINE IT

**I will listen to what others have to say.**
When I wait my turn to speak, I can hear what everyone has to say.

After cutting out the Pledge for Success poster in the Appendix, read the definition aloud together and introduce the importance of listening to your child. Here are some suggestions.

"When we listen, we wait our turn to speak so we can hear

what everyone is saying. Listening is important for adults and kids. When we listen, it shows that we care about each other. It also shows that we can learn from each other. I listen to what you have to say because I care about you. When I go to a meeting with a big group of people, I need to raise my hand if I want to speak, just as you need to raise your hand if you want to speak in your classroom. Think about what happens when everybody talks at once—no one can hear what anyone is saying. We all need to listen to directions the first time they are given to help us at home, at work, and at school."

## 2: EXPERIENCE IT
### Listen Up

Have you ever been introduced to someone and immediately forgot the person's name? We all have at some time or another. Here is a game that helps children practice listening and remembering what they have heard. This game gives us great practice in exercising our listening skill. It's the same skill we need to follow directions or to listen to someone else on the phone.

1. Start by telling the children that you have a game for them that will challenge their ability to listen.

2. Choose a category that you are all familiar with, like colors, numbers, children's names, movies, states, or TV shows.

3. Name a short list (two or three items) from the category and challenge the children to listen and then repeat the list back to you.

4. Have fun with the game. Try it several times with different categories, increasing (or decreasing) the size of the list, depending on the children's ability.

5. Be positive. Remind the children that they are doing a

great job using their listening skills and that they should be proud of themselves.

6. Keep reminding the children that it is all right to make a mistake as long as they are trying their best.

7. Now switch things around. Have children choose a category and ask you to repeat a list. This will show them that adults need to listen just as much as kids do. If other adults are in the room, ask them to try their hand at the game too.

## FURTHER SUGGESTIONS

- If the group is large, ask the children to raise their hands and wait to be called on before they speak. If you're a teacher, this can be a great way to practice and reinforce that students have to raise their hands in the classroom.

After playing the game, discuss the following:

- Think about a time when an adult gave you directions and you listened. What happened?
- Think about a time when an adult gave you directions and you made a mistake and did not listen. What happened?
- When are some times you need to use your listening?

## 3: SHARE IT
### Share Stories About Listening

As you begin to think about sharing from your own life, here are some anecdotes that friends, colleagues, and people from around the country have shared with me. Please share these stories and your own stories about listening, and ask kids to share their stories about listening too.

• • •

A couple I know was on their way to a wedding in an unfamiliar town, and they got lost. After driving in circles for a while, they pulled over and stopped a man walking down the street in order to get directions. The man gave them very detailed directions, mentioning landmarks, the number of stoplights they would pass, and whether the lights were blinking or solid. But when the couple started the car back up, they looked at each other and both said, "Where to?" Neither of them had been paying attention to the directions the man had given. So they had to pull over again, and this time they both listened more carefully to the directions, arriving just as the ceremony was beginning. Both of them remarked that they would have to make a point of listening more carefully in the future.

One day a kindergartner told me that the teacher had given her class a direction, but the girl didn't listen to what it was. When free time started that day, the little girl was overjoyed to see that, for the first time ever, there was no one waiting to use the slide in the corner of the room. So she scampered right up to the top and flung herself down. As she was getting off the slide, though, she landed in the finger paintings that her teacher had put at the bottom of the slide to dry. It turns out that the teacher had given a direction *not* to use the slide during free time for just that reason. The little girl had spattered paint all over the place, and she had to spend the rest of free time cleaning up the floor. She told me that now she tries to listen to everything her teacher says.

## Listening Discussion Starters

A discussion about listening helps children understand that listening plays a major role in their everyday lives. Here are some suggestions.

- Has there ever been a time when you felt you were not listened to? What happened and how did it feel? What about a time when you were listened to? How did that feel?
- How does listening help us in life?
- Discuss some times that listening can keep you safe. (During a fire drill, when you're on a field trip or traveling somewhere in a large group, etc.)

# I Will Treat Others the Way I Would Like to Be Treated

When Effie came into contact with anyone, her face lit up. She said hello as if she had been waiting her whole life just to see you. And it made you feel special, as though you were the only person in the world. Effie treated others the way she liked to be treated. She took her natural love of people and life and used it to relate to others. I know how happy and inspired I felt when she did that. I wanted others to feel that way too. So when we teach the ABCs of Life, we use our natural love for what people say and we do the same things Effie did: We make eye contact and are enthusiastic. This shows others how much pleasure we take in what they say and do. It also shows how much we care.

There is a piece of wisdom that has been passed down through virtually every philosophy and culture in world history: some people call it the Golden Rule. The philosopher Immanuel Kant called it the Categorical Imperative. From the simplest to the most sophisticated, human beings have always understood the basic truth of this concept: People should treat others the way they want to be treated themselves. It's a natural concept that every culture understands; no society lasts long unless its members treat each other with respect. As Abraham Lincoln (quoting an ancient text) said, "A house divided against itself cannot stand." A society whose members do not treat each other as they want to be treated will not survive.

To help kids understand and internalize this crucial idea, we do an activity that requires them to think about a situation from a different perspective. We call this Put Yourself in Someone Else's Shoes. Ask the children to pretend that a new kid has moved into their neighborhood. The new kid doesn't know anyone, and all of the other children in the area don't treat her the way she'd like to be treated: They call her names and push her around. Ask the children how they think the new kid would feel after this kind of treatment. Ask the children if they would want to be treated that way. By being able to put themselves in someone else's shoes and think about how they feel, kids learn empathy and come to understand the importance of treating others the way they would like to be treated.

One mother and teacher, Mary Clain, told me a story about how the Pledge for Success worked in real life. One day, in her classroom, she gave out treats to the kids. One young boy, though, didn't take any. "He was a diabetic," Clain remembers. "He just put his head down on the table; he was very sad. The boy who was handing out the treats was part of the popular clique, but he noticed that this boy wasn't taking anything. He went over and asked him, 'Is there anything on the table that you can eat?'"

Just about every one of us has experienced divisions caused by cliques—in school, at work, on teams, in clubs. In many schools, some cliques conduct a kind of tacit reign of terror, insulting, harassing, sometimes even beating up the kids who are perceived as nerds or geeks or just different. But after learning the Pledge, this popular boy realized the importance of treating others, no matter who they were, the way he would like to be treated, instead of using his social cachet to lord it over other kids.

This reminds me of an incident that occurred when I was in school and having a tough time with biology. The first time I met my friend Roger, he leaned over and told me that he noticed I was having some problems and offered his help. He invited me to his house, where his mother made us ice cream sodas and he tutored me in biology. The thing that amazed me about Roger is that he just wanted to help out of the kindness of his heart. Roger is my friend even to this day. I'm in awe of people like Roger who give of themselves unconditionally.

## Teaching the ABCs of Life: Treating Others Well

### 1: INTRODUCE AND DEFINE IT

**I will treat others the way I would like to be treated.**
Pushing, fighting, bullying, name-calling, and treating others badly hurts them and hurts me.

After cutting out the Pledge for Success poster in the Appendix, read the definition aloud together and introduce the importance of treating others well. Here are some suggestions.

"Treating others the way we would like to be treated is important for adults and kids. When we push other people, fight with them, bully them, call them names, or are just mean to them, we can hurt them, and we can hurt ourselves. When we don't treat others well, it hurts us because we don't feel proud inside. When we are kind to people, share with others, or help them, we are treating them the way they like to be treated. When we do this, we feel proud of ourselves.

"Who is it up to make sure you don't push, fight, bully, or name-call? Of course, it's yourself."

## 2: EXPERIENCE IT
### Put Yourself in Someone Else's Shoes

A new situation can be challenging, whether it's a new school, a new job, or a new home. The following activity asks you to remember this challenge and put yourself in someone else's shoes. In this discussion-based activity, it's important to say how you feel too. So please talk to your child also about how you would respond to these questions.

- Tell your child to pretend that a new kid has moved into your neighborhood. She does not know anyone, but everyone else starts to call her names and push her around. To help your child, ask her to think about a time that she was new to a situation. How did she feel?
- Discuss the following questions:
  —How do you think name-calling and pushing would make the new kid feel? Would you want to be treated that way?
  —How would you feel about yourself if you made someone feel this way?
  —How do we feel when we treat others the way we would like to be treated? Discuss the idea that we want to be *proud* of ourselves; that's why we treat others the way we'd like to be treated.

—Who is it up to to make sure you don't push, bully, or treat others badly?

—Put yourself in the shoes of all of your family members. Think about times when you treated each one the way that you want to be treated. What happened?

—Now think about times you didn't treat them the way you want to be treated. What happened, and what would you do the next time?

FURTHER SUGGESTIONS

- When a situation arises in which a child has not treated others well, take the opportunity to revisit this activity and have him put himself in the other person's shoes to help sensitize him to how it feels from that point of view.

After doing the activity, discuss the following:

- Have you ever been called a name? How did it feel?
- How many people does it take to fight or argue?

## 3: SHARE IT
### Share Stories About Treating Others Well

As you begin to think about sharing from your own life, here are some anecdotes that friends, colleagues, and people from around the country have shared with me. Please share these stories and your own stories about treating others the way you want to be treated, and ask kids to share their stories about treating others the way they want to be treated too.

A friend of mine told me a story about something that happened when he was in first grade. The school he attended had a rule against running on the playground when it was icy. On one icy day, he was following the rule and walking on the playground with a friend of his when he slipped and fell. Before he could get to his feet, a teacher was standing above him and admonishing him for breaking the rule. Without even listening to his explanation, the teacher told him to go the school office. When he went to the principal, the principal didn't listen to his explanation, either. He was told to stand in the hallway until recess was over, while each of his classmates passed by him, one by one. To this day, he wonders how his teacher and principal would have felt if someone had treated them the way they treated him, and he has always tried to treat others like he would want to be treated.

A boy told me a story about a girl in his class who was very quiet and didn't talk to the other students too much. Some of his classmates thought she was a snob. Others just called her weird. And then there were the kids who thought she was just boring and had nothing to say. The boy who was telling me the story said that he started to feel bad for the girl. He mentioned that he thought she might have heard what the other kids were saying about her, and knew that it must be hurtful to hear that sort of thing. So one day the boy went up to her before school and said hi, and to his surprise, she shyly smiled and quietly said hello. They walked to class together, and it turned out that she was just shy and took a while to open up to people. After a while, the two became good friends.

## Treating Others Well Discussion Starters

You and your child can apply the idea of treating others the way you'd like to be treated in your home, school, and community with the following discussion starters.

- How would someone feel if you called him a name, pushed him, or bullied him? How would you feel about yourself if you made someone feel this way?
- What are some examples of treating others the way we would like to be treated?
- How do you feel about yourself when you treat others the way you would like to be treated?
- How can you treat a relative or a friend the way you would like to be treated?
- Think of one person for whom you can go out of your way tomorrow and treat the way you would like to be treated.

# I Will Respect the Diversity of All People

There may be no more compelling theme in American culture than the appreciation of diversity. In works from *Uncle Tom's Cabin* to *Brian's Song*, which taught us that Americans of all races are human, feeling people who can relate to each other at a level that is more than skin-deep, and films like *The Miracle Worker*, *Butterflies Are Free*, and *Awakenings*, which show that people with physical challenges are no different from anyone else, our artistic culture constantly reminds us that diversity is one of the great achievements of our society.

During Boston's desegregation crisis, when I saw the anger and violence unfolding before my eyes, I realized that none of the rock throwers, none of the kids with weapons, would like other people to do to them what they were doing to others. They lacked the skills necessary to understand that other people had the same feelings and the same needs as they did. As I began teaching the earliest versions of the ABCs of Life in Boston schools, I met dozens of children and adults who had never grasped these themes. At the root of the city's social ills was a lack of these skills for dealing with others. Most important, the city was lacking skills for understanding, controlling, and taking responsibility for its own behavior, thoughts, and actions. It didn't have skills to deal with life.

But, as I learned growing up with Effie, the skills don't always reflect the realities of our lives. Too many of us still use racial and ethnic slurs and stereotypes. Women frequently face a glass ceiling in the workplace; adults and children with various learning styles are often being taught in a cookie-cutter manner; people with physical challenges all too often find buildings, public places, and even transportation inaccessible to them, despite laws that make that illegal. When a friend of mine, temporarily in a wheelchair because of a severed Achilles tendon, went to a handicapped-accessible movie theater, he was forced to sit at the top of the stairs and slide down, step by step, because the usher couldn't be bothered to find the keys to the elevator.

In our culture we don't always celebrate the diversity of our interests and ideas. Instead we are told we must be athletes to achieve "success," or that we should wear certain types of clothes to be cool. We can teach children at a young age to celebrate all the hobbies, games, ideas, and interests that they and their friends have. No one taste or activity is more important than another; no one person is better than another.

By showing kids that others—even their closest friends—might have different tastes, ideas, and interests, we teach tolerance and respect. In a game called Celebrating Diversity, they begin to understand why we celebrate diversity and how to do it. Have all the people in a room, kids and adults, play the game. Ask them a simple question about something they might like or not like. For example, some people like apples, others do not.

First, ask those who like apples to raise their hands, then ask those who don't like apples to raise their hands. "Who likes bowling?" might be another question to ask. "Who likes to sing?" could be another. Remind everyone that, instead of ridiculing one another, we can celebrate diversity.

What kids soon realize is that people in their lives have the same or different interests and hobbies. Whether we're the same or different on the outside, kids will learn to understand it's the person who we are on the inside that counts. We all have diverse tastes and ideas, and this game is a lighthearted and enjoyable way of illustrating that fact.

The famous phrase of Martin Luther King, Jr., is one all children and adults can easily learn to take to heart: When we look at others, we should be looking not at the color of their skin but at the content of their character.

## Teaching the ABCs of Life: Respecting Diversity

### 1: INTRODUCE AND DEFINE IT

**I will respect the diversity of all people.**
Whether we are the same or different on the outside, it's the person we are on the inside that counts.

After cutting out the Pledge for Success poster in the Appendix, read the definition aloud together and introduce the importance of respecting diversity. Here are some suggestions.

"I will respect the diversity of all people. Diversity means that people and things can be different. This is easy to remember because the word 'diversity' begins with the letter 'd' and the word 'different' begins with the letter 'd.' Whether we're the same or different on the outside, it's the person we are on the inside that counts. We're proud of who we are, no matter how old we are, what color our skin is, if we're tall or short, wear glasses or not, or speak different languages. It's the type of person we are on the inside that counts. Diversity not only means we look different, it also means that we like different things, wear different clothes, eat different foods, play different sports or not play sports. If people like different things, we don't fight about it, we ask them to tell us about it—and whether we agree or not, we respect one another's differences. Life would be boring if there were only one kind of candy to eat, one movie to watch, or one video game to play. We can like the same thing or different things. It's exciting to celebrate diversity—it's like celebrating at a birthday party."

## 2: EXPERIENCE IT
### Celebrating Diversity

Have you ever tried to express how you feel about what you've seen in a movie or a play, only to find that someone wasn't respecting your point of view? Here is a game in which everyone in the room expresses his or her likes and dislikes in a climate that celebrates everyone's differences and similarities.

1. Start by reviewing the fact that diversity means difference. Explain that we are going to play a game to give us a

chance to celebrate diversity—just as we celebrate a birthday. It would be boring if we were all the same, just as it would be boring if there were only one color in a box of crayons.

2. Ask questions about everyone's likes and dislikes. For example, you might ask who likes to swim. Ask those who like to swim to raise their hands. (Players who like things "a little" can raise their hands partway.) Then ask who does not like to swim. Those who do not like to swim raise their hands. (Even when you're asking the questions, raise your hand when appropriate.)

3. Play the game with different topics. Try ice cream flavors, types of foods, school subjects, sports, hobbies, and other activities. Children and adults can take turns announcing topics.

4. Throughout the game it is important to point out that we are similar in some ways and different in others.

5. As the game is going on, remind children that they are celebrating diversity by not making fun of what other people like or don't like. We all have a tendency sometimes to be judgmental without realizing it. To help reinforce the importance of celebrating diversity, it's important to remind everyone that saying things like "yuck" or "that's stupid" or "I can't believe you like that" is not respecting diversity.

6. Let the children have a chance to make up questions for the game. (In playing this game, make sure nobody mentions other people's names so feelings won't be hurt.)

7. Tell all the children that they have done a great job by celebrating diversity and that they should be proud of themselves.

After playing the game, discuss the following:

- Even if you are the only one who likes something, you have to stand up for what you believe in and celebrate your own diversity. What is something (like a food, movie, or book) you like that you know a lot of other kids don't like? Is it okay to like it?
- How would the world be if everybody looked the same and did all of the same things?
- We're all different and we're proud of who we are. What are some examples of ways we can respect diversity?

Don't assume that certain topics will be liked or disliked by everyone. Not everyone will like ice cream; not everyone will dislike spinach. Topics like these will sometimes produce interesting responses and provide the biggest challenges to accepting diversity.

## 3: *SHARE IT*
### Share Stories About Diversity

As you begin to think about sharing from your own life, here are some anecdotes that friends, colleagues, and people from around the country have shared with me. Please share these stories and your own stories about respecting diversity, and ask kids to share their stories about respecting diversity too.

A woman explained to me that she was a den mother of her son's Cub Scout troop. One little boy in the troop, she said, was confined to a wheelchair. As she planned a hiking trip to the state park, she automatically assumed that the boy in the wheelchair would not be able to come and called the boy's mother to tell her this. But the boy's mother said that a few state parks in the area had handicapped-accessible trails and gave her their phone numbers. Since then, the woman has taken into account all of the options for all of the troop members before making plans for the troop.

I met a boy who loved to dance so much that his parents enrolled him in dancing lessons. He told me all about how his classmates, once they found out about this, started making fun of him, telling him that boys shouldn't dance. When he told his teacher what was going on, she told him that some of the world's most famous dancers were men, like Gene Kelly and Mikhail Baryshnikov. She even showed the class *Singin' in the Rain*, a movie with great dancers in it, both male and female. After seeing the movie, some other boys in the class signed up to take dance lessons too.

## Respecting Diversity Discussion Starters

We have included some ideas for conversations that you and your children can have about diversity, in order to reinforce this topic and give them a point of reference about diversity in their everyday lives.

- How are we different from each other? (We look different and we like different things.)
- How can we respect one another's differences? (by treating others the way we want to be treated)
- What are some examples of celebrating diversity? What is one way you can respect the diversity of a classmate? Of someone at home?

# I Will Remember That I Have People Who Care About Me in My Family, School, and Community

Think about somebody who cared about you at some point in your life. In many cases it was a parent; however, it might have been an aunt or a grandfather. Perhaps a teacher or even a social worker came into your life when you needed help. Families come in all shapes, sizes, and descriptions. Some kids live with two married parents, one or two siblings, and a family dog. But this 1950s vision of the American family is actually in the minority nowadays. Many of the kids we meet live with only one parent, or with grandparents or guardians; they live in blended families, with a stepparent and stepsiblings; they have same-sex parents; they live with adoptive or foster parents. Frequently, they have parents of different ethnic, racial, or religious backgrounds. Once they have learned about diversity, children quickly understand that they should respect others no matter what their families are like. But children need to know that, whatever the state of their families, one family is not better than another. They are people that care about each other.

Just as Effie was there for me, there are teachers and counselors, neighbors and friends, aunts and uncles, and others to whom children can look for guidance. No matter what their family situation, kids need to feel that there are caring adults who will always be there for them, who will help them learn the skills they need to learn so they can care for themselves. When the little girl in Hingham told me that her father had pulled a gun on her, my fellow teachers and I went out of our way to provide a network of caring and support to get her through her crisis. When an angry young boy was hostile to me in Washington, D.C., I learned that his principal and counselors were working on ways to help him cope with a troubled home situation. Sometimes children feel as if they are alone. They feel that no one can help them. We can give children the help they need, whether we are parents, teachers, neighbors, relatives, or friends. We can be the caring adults for these children.

We help kids understand that they have people who care about them and that no family is better than another through the Caring Collage. This activity is based on discussing with kids and adults how different groups of people can be a family and about the importance of remembering that people care for you. For example, you can begin by asking, "If a child lived with her grandfather or her aunt, would she be part of a family?" "If a boy were adopted, would he be part of a family?" Each time, emphasize that these are actual families and that there are many different kinds of families.

The next part of the activity is to have children reflect on people who care about them in their lives. Ask children to make a collage of drawings and photographs of people who care about them in their home, school, and community. This activity gives children proof that they don't ever have to feel alone—their collage is a visual representation of a whole network of people who care about them.

The characters in the film *Lilo and Stich* personify these ideas. When Lilo, a young orphan, expresses her feelings of loneliness, her older sister reminds her, "Family means that nobody gets left behind. Or forgotten." These words cut to the heart of the idea of family—family is not something that's designed to exclude people. Families can include all people, and families can take many different forms; they are made up of people who care about each other. The core of the definition is as simple as that.

As my "mom," Effie taught me that the idea of family is not limited to blood relations. It can be extended to those you care about, no matter who they are: coworkers, friends, teachers. In my life, I seek out people to whom I feel close and include them as members of my family. It's up to you to look for people to make up a healthy family that consists of those who provide feelings of love. If you already have love in your family, you can add to it, to include even more people in a larger extended family. If you come from a family that doesn't provide you with the love you deserve, reach out to your friends, because they can become a part of your new greater family.

Roald Dahl's beloved children's book *Matilda* tells the story of a brilliant young girl with an immense appetite for books and learning. But her parents, Mr. and Mrs. Wormwood, whose main interests include watching television and cheating people out of their money, think that their daughter is a bothersome nuisance. Matilda meets Miss Honey, a young and lonely kindergarten teacher. In Miss Honey, Matilda finds the love that her parents do not provide, and Miss Honey finds the same thing in Matilda. Together they become the family that each of them so desperately needs.

In today's society, in which so many of us spend a great deal of time at work, even coworkers can become caring family members. I recently read an article about a woman who was diagnosed with cancer. Her coworkers sent food and care packages to her house, provided her with babysitting, and held a fund-raiser for her. They couldn't do enough to help her. She said that without their support, she might not have had the strength to fight her disease. How wonderful it must have been for her to feel nurtured and supported by such a large network of caring people. Although these people were not related, they were her family.

After I married and my mother was nearing the end of her life, she gave me one of the few pieces of heartfelt advice I ever got from her: "Never let children interfere with your life." She wasn't saying that to be mean, or even to indicate that she hadn't loved me. In a way, I think she was expressing her love for her son by giving me advice that she thought would help me. The fact is, she never understood that one of the greatest joys any adult can have is to help a child.

You've probably figured out by now that I didn't learn most of what I know about life from my parents. But all those other wonderful adults—Effie, Aunt Fran, Uncle Leon, Mr. Dupee, Mr. Kruger, and Mrs. Simonds, and the rest—were quietly, efficiently, and without my even realizing it at the time filling in the missing pieces of the puzzle. If I couldn't get what I needed for life from my parents, I learned through Effie's influence to find it elsewhere. This is a skill we have to impart to all the children with whom we come in contact.

## Teaching the ABCs of Life:
## Remembering That People Care About You

### 1: INTRODUCE AND DEFINE IT

**I will remember that I have people who care about me in my family, school, and community.**
Families, like schools and communities, can be many sizes and made up of all kinds of people.

After cutting out the Pledge for Success poster in the Appendix, read the definition aloud together and introduce the importance of remembering that people care about you. Here are some suggestions.

"Families can be many sizes and be made up of all kinds of people. There are many different kinds of families. Some kids live with one parent, two parents, grandparents, aunts, uncles, cousins, brothers, sisters, or friends. Some kids are adopted or live in a foster-care situation. Some parents are divorced one or more times. There are other family situations that are unique to other people's lives. No one family is better than another. Families are made up of people who care about each other. And most important, remember that you have people who care about you in your life. I care about you. And there is someone who is with you all the time who cares about you—yourself. We're both learning skills so that we can care about ourselves and others."

## 2: *EXPERIENCE IT*
### Caring Collage

We have people who care about us in a variety of areas in our lives: family members, husbands, wives, children, girlfriends, boyfriends, coworkers, friends. We do this activity to help children internalize the idea that they too have many people who care about them and how important it is to remember this fact.

1. Ask kids the following questions: If kids live with an uncle and aunt, is that a family? If kids live in a foster situation, is that a family? If kids live with a stepparent, is that a family? (We encourage you to mention other examples too.)
2. Together, think about people who care about you. These

can be people in your families, schools, workplaces, and communities.

3. Have children make a collage of drawings and/or photographs of people who care about them in their homes, schools, and communities. Make a collage yourself, to show the importance of the idea of having people that care about you, no matter what your age.

4. Together, look at the collages you have made—illustrations of all the people who care about you both.

5. Children can interview the people they draw in their pictures and ask them about the people who cared about them when they were young.

After doing this activity, discuss the following:

- If you are working with a group, some of the collages might have more people than others. Discuss how it doesn't matter how many people you have. What's important is the kind of people you have and what they're like on the inside.

- How is your family different from other families? Is that okay?

- Discuss why it is important to remember that people care about you.

## 3: *SHARE IT*
### Share Stories About Remembering That People Care About You

As you begin to think about sharing from your own life, here are some anecdotes that friends, colleagues, and people from around the country have shared with me. Please share these stories and your own stories about remembering that people care about you, and ask kids to share their stories about remembering that people care about you too.

One of my coworkers comes from a family that doesn't get together to celebrate the holidays. She admits that this makes her feel lonely at times. But whenever she feels this way, she tries to remind herself that family isn't just a group of relatives. A lot of her friends invite her over to celebrate holidays with them and their families. Sometimes, she gets so many invitations that she doesn't know which one to accept. It's great that she has so many people who care about her.

At a workshop that I conducted recently, a boy told this story. When his parents divorced, his dad moved to another state, and the boy didn't have the chance to see him very often. The boy didn't have anyone to play football or soccer with because his mother didn't enjoy playing those sports. But then his mother signed him up for a group that matched him up with a "big brother" from a nearby college. They go to the park to play ball together almost every weekend. The boy beamed as he said that his big brother had even taken him to a professional-football game. Even though his big brother is not his father or his relative, the boy said that it still feels like he's a family member because they care about each other so much.

## Remembering That People Care About You
### Discussion Starters

A conversation about the people who care about you will really solidify this idea for kids. Here are some suggestions to get kids talking.

- Talk with your child about the fact that families are made up of people who care about you; in turn, you care about them. No one family is better than another.
- Have a discussion about the people you know personally who care about you. Also discuss the importance of knowing that the person who will always be there for you is yourself.
- Discuss people in your community who care about people—firefighters, crossing guards, bus drivers, and doctors are examples.

# I Will Try My Best

I cringe whenever I go to a movie about young people—so-called slackers—whose response to any challenge, chore, school assignment, or request is to shrug and mumble "whatever." Popular culture has begun to glorify the notion that to be cool, young people have to be disaffected and disenchanted, that they should put out the least possible effort to make it through a day. Movies, TV shows, and music convey the message that young people should try their least. We owe it to our kids to teach them to try their best.

While working on my master's program, I had an assignment that took me until two A.M. to complete. The next day, I went to work after only a few hours of sleep. While teaching a lesson, I kept making all sorts of mistakes because I was so tired. I held up a pencil and called it a piece of paper; I almost missed my chair (it was on wheels) when I sat down. Just when I thought things couldn't get worse, I noticed that the kids were laughing. Shy children were raising their hands to correct me. The whole class was filled with excitement, but also relief. I didn't realize that the children felt good seeing an adult make mistakes. It reminded them then it was okay for them to make mistakes.

I remember watching old episodes of Abbott and Costello reciting their classic "Who's on First" routine, Laurel and Hardy bringing a piano through a window when the door was open, Dick Van Dyke tripping over the ottoman, and Lucy and Ethel stuffing chocolates in their dresses, in their hats, and in their mouths so that they could keep up with a conveyor belt. These scenes took me away from feeling inferior at my studies and rejected by my parents. There were people making even bigger mistakes than I did; I learned to laugh at myself. On that day long ago, I think the students felt the same way. This was a breakthrough, and one of the most exciting days of my life. From then on, I have incorporated activities about making mistakes as an integral part of living and working with children.

Trying our best brings out the humanity in everyone. Our culture tells us that even if we try our best, it's not okay to make mistakes. Yet there is a universal quality and appeal to the scenes I've just described. People identify with people who make mistakes and realize that they are not alone. Everyone makes mistakes. We can't put ourselves down about it. It's okay to laugh at ourselves. That's what the ABCs of Life are all about: creating a climate of joy in our culture.

When we make mistakes, we should think about what we can learn from them for the next time. Did we really try our best? It's important to admit to our mistakes and be honest about them in order to learn from them. With any of the skills, we can't grow or change until we're honest with ourselves and can reflect on how we did or did not use them. And as long as we tried our very best to do something, we can look back and feel that we've been successful.

We introduce the idea that mistakes are okay by using a drum and a drumstick in a simple game called the Drumroll Shake. Ask all the people in the room to raise their hands. Tell them to shake their hands whenever you are pounding the drum but hold still when you stop. You can make it fun by stopping short before striking it again. Some people will make mistakes, others won't, but that's okay, as long as everyone is trying his or her best.

This game sends a powerful message: It's all right to make mistakes. As adults, many of us are afraid of making mistakes because of lessons we learned in childhood, but we should all ask ourselves: How do you learn if you don't make mistakes? We are trying to shift the model by which kids and adults learn to be proud of themselves; we are telling them that they don't have to be perfect to be proud. They need to know that they have tried their best.

The first effect on a child or adult who fully understands that it's okay to make a mistake is a feeling of liberation. All of us can remember being scolded, reprimanded, or even physically punished as children when we made mistakes. One woman I met was forced to sit in a corner in full view of her classmates for making a mistake. A grown man still remembers how his father slapped him when he tripped and dropped a small carton of milk.

These experiences do more than leave psychological scars; they teach us to judge ourselves harshly when we fall short of our goals. Rather than learning to do our best and be content on those occasions—which all of us have—when our best isn't 100 percent perfect, we learn to be angry with ourselves, even to hate ourselves, if we don't achieve perfection every time.

One teacher told me a story about how the piano teacher from whom she took lessons as a child poked her with knitting needles every time she made a mistake. She came to detest playing the piano, because she was so afraid of making a mistake. So she quit. But after talking to her class about trying her best and internalizing the ABCs of Life, she decided to start taking piano lessons again. She let her class know that she didn't want her fear of one teacher to keep her from doing something that she had enjoyed.

I have talked with countless adults who were so shattered by the fear of doing something wrong that they gave up or didn't even try to do activities they would enjoy. We are taught at an early age that we have labels attached to us: We are dumb or smart, talented or untalented, athletic or unathletic—the list goes on. From this point on, we judge ourselves and often become paralyzed by the idea of trying new things. We can break this image when we really believe that it is okay to make mistakes and relish the simple joy of trying our best. By focusing on the process of the activity, rather than success or failure, we can begin to take risks and expand ourselves farther than we thought possible.

Think of Thomas Edison. Working away in his laboratory in Menlo Park, New Jersey, he was convinced that he could create an electric device that would provide light. But he needed to run electricity through a filament—that little wire inside the bulb that glows and gives off light. For months he tried every material he could think of—iron, steel, copper, you name it. None of them worked. Then he decided to try a relatively unusual element called tungsten, which, more than a century later, is the material in most incandescent lightbulbs today. He wasn't afraid to make one mistake after another after another. Each time he made a mistake, he learned something new. All those mistakes led to the right answer.

I ask all the adults in the classroom to share with the kids the kinds of stories teachers rarely tell their students—how they got distracted and put cereal in the dog's bowl and dog food in their own bowl, locked themselves out of the house, or were in a hurry and put on two different shoes. I get the ball rolling by telling them about parking my car near a skunk's den—it reeked for weeks. The point, which kids instantly grasp, is that it's all right to make mistakes, as long as you're trying your best.

Many of us are afraid of trying new things. We wear the type of clothes the people around us wear; we drive the kinds of cars they drive. Rather than striking out on our own, we stay in jobs we don't like because they confer social status on us. Fear of being different, fear of the new, fear of failure, are powerful emotions in our culture. We are afraid that people will make fun of us if we make mistakes. We are afraid to try our best.

In my childhood apartment in Brooklyn, the walls were paper-thin. My father's medical office was separated from my bedroom by one of these walls. When I was learning to play the trumpet as a kid, my father's patients would either applaud my trumpet-playing skills, make requests, or yell through the wall that I was helping my father's business by giving all of them headaches. After a while, I played only the songs that I knew I would not make mistakes at because I didn't want to be heckled. Afraid of making mistakes, I never reached my full potential as a trumpet player. I let external influences keep me from practicing.

What if Picasso and Braque had not taken the plunge into Cubism? Art would not be the same. What if Billy Mitchell had not told his superiors in the army that the airplane was the next great invention? He was court-martialed for it, but he is now seen as a visionary. What if Agnes de Mille had not decided to break all the rules of choreography and give us *Oklahoma!*? Or Langston Hughes hadn't broken the rules of traditional poetry?

Breaking free of fear—fear of criticism, fear of ridicule, fear of being different—is crucial to doing your best.

A while back, I visited New York for the annual toy show. I attend every year for two reasons: I constantly find new toys that I can use as learning tools, and I have a blast. The show gives me a chance to be childlike, not childish, and look with wonder at all the ingenious new devices people have invented to bring fun into other people's lives.

On this trip, my hotel room wasn't ready when I got there, and when I got it, it wasn't clean. Politely, I reported these problems to the front desk. That's how I came to meet a man named David Bird, the general manager of the Roosevelt Hotel. He immediately took ownership of the mistake and upgraded me to a suite. As we spoke, he explained his philosophy of managing to me.

"Our people work very hard," he said, "and, when something like this happens, it's usually not because somebody did something wrong on purpose. There's usually a problem in our system. We try not to blame people; that doesn't help them or me. We expect to make mistakes a part of daily life. In our meetings, we discuss the mistakes we've made and talk about what we can do to avoid those mistakes in the future. Everyone makes mistakes. It's important to focus on the process that brings about change."

By instituting a policy that is aimed at fixing problems rather than assessing blame, Bird encourages people to try their best.

They are not afraid to make a mistake. In this pleasant atmosphere, people who work there feel accepted, wanted, and needed, and they work hard so that the hotel's guests feel the same way. The guests at the hotel experience the sensation of visiting a home away from home. Bird is applying to grown-ups in the workplace the same philosophy we try to apply to kids: Praise them when they try their best, don't punish them when they make honest mistakes. It's no wonder he has cut employee turnover in his tenure as boss.

As I travel around the country, I hear many stories from parents about community events. One mother told me about a soccer game she attended where the players ranged from the ages of seven to ten. The coach had a strict policy of giving every child a chance to play and rotating a child into every position. This is a very good way of encouraging children to try their best; if they make a mistake, they get another chance next week. A tie had developed toward the end of this game. The team member whose turn it was to play goalie was a boy with just one arm. The coach sent him in at goal. He didn't block a shot, and his team lost. (The way she described it, it didn't sound as if the Hindu deity Vishnu, with all four of his arms, could have blocked the shot.)

The coach and the team members were happy with their performance, but their pride in trying their best wasn't shared by some of their parents. An angry line of allegedly mature adults marched up to the coach and excoriated him for letting this boy with one arm play goalie. Altogether too many children learn this lesson from their parents: Winning is the only thing.

Perhaps these grown-ups should have learned a lesson from their kids.

# Teaching the ABCs of Life: Trying Your Best

## 1: INTRODUCE AND DEFINE IT

**I will try my best.**
Even when I make mistakes, I learn from them.
The most important thing is to keep trying.

After cutting out the Pledge for Success poster in the Appendix, read the definition aloud together and introduce the importance of trying our best. Here are some suggestions.

"We can try our best at everything we do. Even when we make a mistake, the most important thing is to keep trying. Everyone makes mistakes. Adults make mistakes just like kids do. When we make one, we don't have to put ourselves down about it. Instead, you and I can remind ourselves that it's okay to make a mistake. Mistakes are an opportunity for us to learn more. And after we make a mistake and have learned from it, we can also try our best not to make the mistake again. You and I both can try our best no matter what we're doing, when you're at school and I'm at work, when we play games together, when we play musical instruments, when we play sports, or even when we follow the Pledge for Success. Together, we can make this a regular part of our lives."

## 2: *EXPERIENCE IT*

### Drumroll Shake

Have you ever made a mistake and put yourself down so much that it affected the rest of the day? Mistakes are a part of life; we make them all the time. We all need to learn that it is okay to make mistakes as long as we are trying our best. We can just feel proud because we tried our best, and we can learn from our mistakes.

1. Tell the children that you will be playing a game about trying your best and how it's okay to make mistakes. To play this game you can use a drum, a tambourine, or even a pot and wooden spoon.

2. Explain that when you hit the drum, children should shake their hands in the air, but when you don't hit the drum, children should try their best to keep their hands still. It is important that the children shake their hands *when* you are hitting the drum, not *after* you make the sound.

3. As you play the game, hit the drum in a variety of ways. Hit it quickly, then slowly, and urge the children to shake their hands at a corresponding speed. Stop suddenly before hitting the drum to make the game more challenging. Bring your own personality into the game and play it in a variety of ways.

4. Remind children when they make a mistake that it is okay as long as they are trying their best.

5. It's important to talk to children about not comparing themselves to others. Tell the children that they should be proud of themselves even if they made a mistake.

6. Now switch roles and ask a child to lead the game. This will show the children in a very tangible way that adults make mistakes too.

## Hand-Clap Game

In life we all deal with challenging situations. We can either choose to give up or try our best and learn from them. This exciting yet simple game challenges children to try their best.

1. Tell the children that they will be playing a challenging game about trying their best and that in this game it's okay if they make a mistake just as it's okay if they make a mistake while trying their best on a test, playing a sport, or playing a musical instrument.
2. Put your hands in front of you with your palms facing each other, as if you are going to clap your hands. Ask children to watch your hand movements and try their best to clap along with you.
3. The challenge of the game is to have the kids clap their hands *when* you clap your hands, not *before* you clap or *after* you clap, so start slowly and make sure that children are clapping their hands at the same time you are.
4. Have fun and vary the speed of your claps. After a few times, stop short before your hands meet or have your hands miss each other to challenge children's ability to follow you.
5. Remind them not to feel frustrated and give up if they make a mistake. This game is about trying their best.
6. Congratulate them all on trying their best and tell them that they should be proud of themselves.
7. Now switch roles and ask a child to lead the game by clap-

ping his or her hands while you try to clap with them, which will show them that everyone makes mistakes.

After playing both games, discuss the following:

- Did you make a mistake during the games?
- If we are trying our best, is it okay to make a mistake?
- What should you do if you make a mistake?
- Talk about how trying your best relates to other activities like playing sports, playing a video game, learning something new at school, or even cleaning your room.

## 3: SHARE IT

### Share Stories About Trying Your Best

As you begin to think about sharing from your own life, here are some anecdotes that friends, colleagues, and people from around the country have shared with me. Please share these stories and your own stories about trying your best, and ask kids to share their stories about trying their best too.

One teacher told me a story about America's national pastime: baseball. He hadn't liked the sport as a child, but when he had a son, he unearthed his childhood mitt so they could play together. His son loved to play and signed them up for a parent-and-child baseball game. The man said that he was so nervous that he had visions of being the only adult to bat .000. As the day approached, he grew more and more anxious, convincing himself that he would miss every ball that came his way and strike out at every at bat. But on game day, he just tried his best and actually had fun in the process. He missed some balls, but he caught some too. He struck out a few times, but he had a hit.

And at the end of the game, he felt great, because he had tried his best, just as he had always told his son to do.

Friends of mine went on a family vacation and stayed in a sprawling two-story hotel. One of their daughters told me a story about one early morning when she and her sister left their second-floor room to go to the ice machine on the first floor. On their way back to their room, they knocked on the door they thought was their parents' room. They knocked and knocked, but their parents didn't answer. Finally, a woman with blond hair in curlers and a bathrobe came to the door, looking very confused and sleepy! The girls had thought they were knocking on the door of room 212, but they were actually standing at the door of room 112. Since then, the two sisters have tried their best to pay attention to where they are going.

## Trying Your Best Discussion Starters

Making mistakes and trying your best are a natural part of the reality of our daily lives. We include some discussion starters to reinforce the idea that it's okay to make a mistake, as long as we learn from it and continue to try our best.

- If people make fun of you when you make a mistake, even though you tried your best, should you still be proud of yourself? Why?
- Should you make fun of people who make mistakes? What should you do instead?
- What are some mistakes you have made? What did you learn from them? What will you do the next time?
- When are times you have to try your best and not give up?
- What should you do if you make a mistake? How can you help yourself learn from your mistakes?

## Teaching the Pledge for Success

On television and in the newspapers, we hear stories about people who try their best in academics, in the arts, in sports, in politics, in every area of human endeavor. When they do this, they feel proud of themselves. These people have learned the ABCs of Life, and they follow the Pledge for Success. When we talk about the Pledge for Success, we talk about skills we all need to practice so that we can feel proud of ourselves, as kids and adults.

When we make a promise to ourselves—any promise, no matter whether it involves food, exercise, or the amount of work we plan to get done—and we keep it all day long, we feel proud of ourselves. The same principle applies with this Pledge. When we follow the Pledge for Success, we have a lot of reasons to feel proud of ourselves.

## Pledge for Success Skill Builders for Adults and Children

The parts of the Pledge for Success are universal; therefore, you can apply them to a variety of things you see in your daily lives. In your discussions, you can include current events, movies, books, or historical happenings.

- What part of the Pledge for Success do you feel you need to improve in most (e.g., listening, trying, etc.)? What can you do to help yourself in that area?
- Have a conversation about role models—people you know—who follow various aspects of the the Pledge for Success. For example, you might have a cousin who respects diversity or a neighbor who cares about you.
- The skills are everywhere. Give an example of a book, movie, current event, or television show where people or

characters either used or didn't use different aspects of the Pledge for Success. For example, in the *Jungle Book*, some of the jungle animals cared for Mowgli as if he were a member of their family. And in *Toy Story*, throughout their adventures, Woody and Buzz had to learn to treat others the way they liked to be treated.

## Pledge for Success Helpful Hints

It's important to read both sentences in each part of the Pledge for Success. The first sentence explains the promise you make, then the second sentence explains why you make that promise.

After you have introduced the Pledge for Success to children, find a time to talk about aspects of the Pledge. For example, at the dinner table or before bedtime you can read the Pledge and talk about how each of you used (or didn't use) an aspect of the Pledge. Classroom teachers nationwide have found it useful to start the day by reading the Pledge aloud with their students. Find a mutually convenient time to go over the Pledge for Success. This is a quick and effective way of making sure you and your child will keep the promise throughout the day.

All ABCs of Life games can be played in a variety of settings. For example, while waiting on line at a grocery store or during a car trip, you can play Listen Up to help children practice listening. You can use categories such as fruit, dairy products, cities, farm animals—virtually anything. A coach can play the Hand-Clap game before a sports competition, or a teacher can play the Drum Roll Shake before a test to help children remember the importance of trying their best.

You can use the Pledge for Success as a point of reference and an integrated part of your life by referring to each of its aspects. It is important to be positive and notice when your children are doing a good job. Remind them that they're keeping the promise they made to themselves to follow the Pledge for Success. If they need to improve in some areas, remind them of the Pledge. You can talk to them about how they can learn from their mistakes and try their best to follow the Pledge the next time. Tell them that the reason we follow the Pledge for Success is that it makes us feel good about who we are.

When children have a basic understanding of the Pledge for Success and they've learned to take ownership of the Pledge, they're ready to learn the rest of the skills. The Pledge for Success is the foundation on which the skills are built; the skills, in turn, are the foundation for a healthy, productive, happy life.

$$\sim\quad\sim\quad\sim$$

The Pledge for Success is a valuable prerequisite for a civil society.

Listen to what others have to say, and what happens? We become friends; we don't squabble with our neighbors over unimportant boundary disputes; we don't fight in the playground. On a global scale, we go to the United Nations or the World Court and work out our differences civilly.

And if we don't listen to each other? Bloody noses, lawsuits, killings, and even war are the result. Therefore:

I WILL LISTEN TO WHAT OTHERS HAVE TO SAY.
*When I wait my turn to speak, I can hear what everyone has to say.*

Treat others as they would like to be treated, and what happens? The answer is as old as Socrates: They will treat you the same way. In Aesop's fable, the mouse who pulled the thorn from the lion's paw was rewarded not only by not being eaten; later, the lion helped the mouse.

Treat others harshly, and you can expect the same in return. Just think of classic movies from *Spartacus* to *Cool Hand Luke* to *Taps*. In each of them, people were treated unfairly—whether slaves in ancient Rome, prisoners in the South, or students at a military school. Because they were not treated as all of us would like to be treated, they rebelled and lashed back with violence. Therefore:

**I WILL TREAT OTHERS THE WAY I WOULD LIKE TO BE TREATED.**
*Pushing, fighting, bullying, name-calling, and treating others badly hurts them and hurts me.*

What happens when we respect diversity? People like Nelson Mandela bring together fellow citizens of different races and they construct a modern nation. People like Mairead Corrigan and Betty Williams bring together people of different religions and they help reduce the violence in Northern Ireland. People like Mother Teresa devote their lives to helping the world's poorest people, of all religions and many different ethnicities. They all won the Nobel Peace Prize because they respected people of different backgrounds and worked together with them to make their cultures better.

You don't have to be a world-famous figure or a Nobel Peace Prize winner to make respecting diversity a reality in your family or community. You can belong to any race or religion, any nation or ethnic group. The message resonates throughout human society. Nelson Mandela gained the respect of his white wardens at Robben Island who admired him for his dignity, his decency, and his nonviolence; Gandhi won the admiration of the British imperial administrators who at first tried to suppress him; the Hebrew prophet Micah asked, "What does the Lord require of you, but to love justice and act mercifully?"; the Christian Francis of Assisi said, "Where there is hatred let me sow love, where there is darkness, light. Grant that I may not so much seek to be loved as to love."

These words and deeds have echoed through the ages, from various places and cultures, because we all instinctively understand how true they are. We know in our hearts that we should respect diversity. The world will be a better place when we all do.

And if we don't? In Texas, two men dragged an innocent man to his death behind a pickup truck for the simple reason that he was black. In Wyoming, two men tortured a college student and left him to die, tied to a barbed-wire fence, because he was gay. In Detroit, some American automobile workers beat a Chinese-American man to death because they thought he was Japanese, a citizen of a country that competed with their employer. The world now lives in fear of terrorism, because huge segments of the population can't understand and respect each other's differences. Therefore:

I WILL RESPECT THE DIVERSITY OF ALL PEOPLE.
*Whether we are the same or different on the outside, it's the person we are on the inside that counts.*

When most children have problems, questions, or trouble, they can turn to one or both parents for help. But some kids learn early on that they need to find aunts or uncles, grandparents, teachers, neighbors, or others to help them out. In every community, there are adults who care about kids. Once we are grown up ourselves, we know that we can go to a firefighter or police officer if there's an emergency, and to a spouse, companion, or friend if we have troubles. It is important that we communicate to kids that they too have people who care, who will help them. And, above all, we need to remind them that they will always have themselves.

What happens if we don't? The newspapers are littered with stories about desperate young people who left behind suicide notes saying that nobody cared about them. Others take out their anger in outbursts of violence at school or at home. Some slowly destroy themselves with drugs or alcohol. Imagine what a world of peace and friendship we could live in if we raised a whole generation that knew it always had someone to turn to for help. Therefore:

**I WILL REMEMBER THAT I HAVE PEOPLE WHO CARE ABOUT ME IN MY FAMILY, SCHOOL, AND COMMUNITY.**
*Families, like schools and communities, can be many sizes and made up of all kinds of people.*

How do you try your best? Well, one good definition is to give your all to everything you do; then, if you don't achieve your goal, try it again. Louis L'Amour, one of the best-selling authors of all time, was rejected two hundred times before he was published. Beatrix Potter's first book was turned down so often that she published it herself. It was called *The Tale of Peter Rabbit*.

You try your best by being prepared, as well. One of baseball's most successful pitchers, Nolan Ryan, built a gym for himself on his Texas ranch and worked out there for hours every day during the winter off-season. His career lasted a decade longer than most pitchers'. Yo-Yo Ma spent his childhood practicing the cello and ended up with a worldwide reputation and concert career. I have a friend who practiced the clarinet for years but never became a superstar; instead he taught music in high school and brought pleasure and art into the lives of hundreds of kids. I know another guy who almost made it as a professional hockey player; he didn't get to the NHL, but he has helped dozens of kids to learn and enjoy the sport. The fame, the money, the roar of the crowd are all very nice. But it's the internal satisfaction of a job well done and a giving back to the community that create real happiness. Therefore:

I WILL TRY MY BEST.
*Even when I make mistakes, I learn from them. The most important thing is to keep trying.*

In a school in Ohio, a boy approached his principal and talked to her about his life. He was from a single-parent family; he was home alone often, because his father worked overtime in a struggle to make ends meet. His older brother didn't provide him with much companionship, the boy said. In fact, his brother often beat him up. Then he asked the principal for a copy of the Pledge for Success in a small size that he could carry with him. Although the school gave copies of the Pledge to all the children to put on their refrigerators, the principal was in awe that this boy wanted his own copy to help him take charge of his difficult situation. The boy knew that the Pledge wasn't going to solve the problems he was experiencing at home, but it would remind him of the choices he would have by using the skills.

# 5

# Self-Control

Self-control is the most basic of the skills. Without it, some of us might not even get out of bed in the morning. Think about it:

Getting ready for work or school: It takes self-control (and sometimes a lot of it) not to hit the snooze button and go back to sleep.

Studying or focusing on a job: It's easy to find distractions if we allow ourselves to do so; this lack of self-control is a common problem.

Interrupting people: Although it's common courtesy to hear people out, many people become so excited about expressing their own thoughts that they can't wait until someone else has completed a sentence before they begin speaking.

Anger: Sometimes people lose their self-control and let their anger take over. We see this in road rage and airplane rage (when people are so hostile to the cabin crew or even their fellow airline passengers that they are arrested when they disembark from the plane). Domestic abuse, as well as other types of physical and mental abuse, is in the news every day.

Addictions: Whether to food, alcohol, shopping, cigarettes, or drugs, addictions are real and harmful. When people don't use their self-control and drink and then decide to drive, the consequences are often deadly, or at least tragic. Lives can be ruined or destroyed. Countless deaths occur because of overdoses of drugs or alcohol.

Overreacting: We've all dealt with rude salespeople, people who cut in line, snooty waitstaff at restaurants, and people who elbow their way through a crowd without saying "Excuse me." Lashing out at them is no answer to their behavior; in fact, it can make it worse and lead us into aggressive behavior we may later regret.

Impulsive violence: Every day's newspaper in any large city contains stories of young people—and sometimes not-so-young people—who pulled out a knife or a gun at a club or a party and attacked someone whom they perceived as disrespectful to them. Without self-control, it's easy to ruin two lives in one momentary outburst.

> *Self-control is when I control what I do and what I say. I use my self-control to follow directions. Using self-control helps me resist doing things that may be harmful to myself and others. Self-control helps me stay safe and be successful.*

Self-control is a crucial skill in the ABCs of Life that cannot be taught as a punitive measure or instilled by intimidation or discipline from outside. In their very earliest years, kids can learn self-control through the enjoyable exercises we teach.

Early on, we make it clear to children that self-control is not a punishment; rather, it is both fun and empowering. Immediately, we tell the children that self-control is a skill that we can use to keep ourselves safe and successful. By using it, we learn to follow directions, control what we say and do, and resist doing things that might harm ourselves and others.

I was in graduate school when I learned the lesson that lies at the base of Lesson One's way of teaching self-control. In studying for my master's degree, I took a course in dance therapy. The professor had us move to the beat of a drum; when the drumbeat stopped, we were all supposed to cease all movement. She repeated the exercise several times, then posed a simple question: "Who made you move?"

"You did," some of the students said.

"I didn't come over to you and move your hands for you," she said.

"The drum did," others offered.

"The drum didn't come over to you and move your hands for you," she reminded us.

"Who made you move?" she asked again.

Then someone answered, "We made ourselves move."

That's self-control. It was a breakthrough for me, for my fellow students, and for Lesson One.

After the article about Lesson One appeared in *Parade* magazine, we received letters from all over the country—in fact, from every state. The letters that really moved me came from prison inmates who said they wished that they had learned these skills when they were kids. Many of these men and women are behind bars today because they went along with friends who involved them in robberies, burglaries, carjackings, and even murders. In the criminal-justice system, "my friend made me do it" is not a valid alibi for crime; only you can control yourself. Lesson One struck a chord throughout the nation, because violence, acting out, rage, and bad behavior have become endemic in our culture; we offered a way to stop them.

The film *Willy Wonka and the Chocolate Factory* comments on the lack of self-control in society. The child characters lack self-control: Augustus Gloop is prone to gluttony, Veruca Salt is a spoiled kid, Violet Beauregarde is a know-it-all gum addict, and Mike Teevee's eyes never stray from the television set. Until the day they enter Willy Wonka's factory, the children's cheeky behavior and lack of self-control are allowed to go unchecked. Why? Their parents lack self-control too, and they don't set limits, and so the conduct becomes a cycle.

Although this film seems lighthearted, it actually provides a resonant social commentary about self-control; situations like this are everywhere in our culture. Perhaps this is one of the reasons the film is so popular: Kids and adults identify with it. Parents are trying their best, but sometimes they don't set limits for kids because they have never been taught how to do it. And children see some of themselves in the movie's characters. Children and adults crave that same limit-setting and structure that the characters in the film so badly need. For generations, parents have been trying their best with limit-setting and children have been craving structure.

In his wonderful musical *Into the Woods*, Stephen Sondheim has a character sing:

> *Careful the things you say,*
> *Children will listen.*
> *Careful the things you do,*
> *Children will see.*
> *And learn.*

This is a poetic statement of a profound truth: Kids watch what we do, and they imitate our behavior. Every adult should be an example of self-control to every child. A child who sees one adult abuse another may well grow up to be an abuser or a seriously traumatized adult herself. A child who hears intemperate words learns how to use them himself. Our behavior must match our teachings; we must communicate to children that self-control is serious. It's not punitive, it's not onerous, but it's a skill that we all must practice every day.

Self-control is something that people of all ages can learn. Even at a very young age, kids understand self-control if it's properly explained to them and backed up with games and stories that flesh out the idea. We use games and stories that help kids to internalize the ideas in a way that is fun and nonthreatening.

I get excited when I see that children have internalized the skills. One day while I was teaching, a girl raised her hand to tell me about something that happened relating to self-control. While riding in the family car with her mother, they were rearended by another car in a minor fender bender. The person who ran into them insisted to the police officer who came to the scene that the accident was not his fault. He argued that the other car made him bump into it. In fact, as the girl had observed, he had not been paying attention and caused the accident himself.

The girl asked the officer how the collision could not have been the man's fault. After just learning about self-control in her school, she told the officer that they didn't make him bump into them, he made himself do it. He was the one in control of himself and his vehicle. The officer was fascinated that a child this young had the capability to analyze the situation in such a way. She really internalized the skill of self-control.

Now, as I've already mentioned, one of the most important

things we try to instill in the ABCs of Life is the awareness of how important it is for all of us to treat other people as we would like to be treated.

A third-grader in the back of the room raised his hand when I asked the children for examples of how they had used self-control in their lives. His story moved me. This young boy was a victim of the unthinking cruelty of some older kids who had not had the self-control lesson. On the school bus the afternoon before, a number of other children began taunting him, calling him abusive names. You could sense the hurt and anger he felt in his voice and his movement as he told the story. But he was sitting up straight and obviously was proud when he told the class how he had not taken the bait and lashed out. Instead, he waited until the bus stopped, then told an adult about his problem. He didn't scream or tease or hit the kids who were victimizing him.

It wasn't easy, he admitted. He was very angry. But he had learned that self-control is something he could do for himself, not for others. No one could make him lash out. No one could make him taunt or tease or use rough language.

After that class, the boy's teacher took me aside and told me what moviemakers call the backstory, the history of this boy's dealings with the older kids who were picking on him. He had been in many physical fights with them; name-calling and yelling were common occurrences. The teacher, the guidance counselor, and the principal were concerned about the situation. So were the boy's parents, who had been in contact with the school about it. Before he learned about self-control, the boy used the same old explanations every time he got into a fistfight: "He made me do it" or "They made me do it."

Of course, he was justified in being upset that other kids were treating him in a manner that was totally unacceptable. Using self-control doesn't mean condoning the unjust acts of others. But learning about self-control changed his perspective. He no longer blamed the bullies for getting him into fights. He came to realize that, no matter what other people did, he was the master of his own behavior. He also learned the importance of sharing his feelings.

This is a perfect example of why the message of Lesson One carries such urgency. What would have happened if this boy had not had this revelation? What happens to all the children who don't? They hold their feelings in, and these feelings manifest themselves in society. They resurface in many forms: from bullying to school shootings, from road rage to domestic violence. Sometimes decades go by before the repressed feelings come out. The children who had experiences like those of this third-grader can suffer for the rest of their lives. And the question isn't whether they are going to explode from their feelings; the question is when they're going to do it.

Eleanor Roosevelt famously remarked that nobody can make you feel inferior without your cooperation. This boy came to understand that nobody could make him act badly without his cooperation. That morning in class, he proudly spoke about how good he felt when he used his self-control to avoid a fight, rather than mixing it up with the bullies. It was hard for him to restrain himself, to contain his anger and use self-control, but he did it, and he ended the cycle of victimization.

I've heard dozens of stories like this from around the country. Teachers and parents, adults and kids, constantly tell me how they have used their self-control to improve the quality of their lives. Kids have told me about walking away from drugs, not stealing, and even avoiding junk foods before meals. When adults share their stories in classrooms and at home, they talk about thinking twice before getting into arguments, planning ahead to get to work on bad weather days, even avoiding being overbearing to their kids at athletic contests.

"If I don't leave a restaurant feeling like I gorged myself," a friend of mine once told me, "I don't feel that I've got my money's worth." How many times have we gone into a restaurant, been confronted by a plate of food, and eaten long past the point of being full because, as George Mallory said of climbing Mount Everest, "It was there"? Instead of trusting ourselves to gauge when we are done, we abandon our self-control and eat until our plate is clean. We base our food intake on an external— the amount of food the restaurant provided—instead of trusting ourselves to use our self-control. We base much of our behavior on the behavior of others. If everyone else orders dessert, we tend to do likewise, even if we know we need to diet.

My brother Mark and I once visited an all-you-can-eat steak and seafood restaurant. This was an event that we had been planning for a long time; both of us had been "in training" and had fasted for the day. We went to the restaurant knowing that we should skip the soup and bread, to avoid filling ourselves up too much before we ate the steak and lobsters. When we were looking for the restaurant, we recognized it because, on a warm day, there were people lying on their backs outside, like basking seals who have overfed themselves. We asked each other how people could be such gluttons. Our question was soon answered. We ate and ate (my brother ate at least twelve lobsters—they were small). By the end, we were simply eating to say how much we'd eaten. We started playing with our food; we set up games in which the lobsters and steak talked to each other. As we ate, we added up how much money we were making from our savings on the meal. And when we left the restaurant, we had to take a few minutes to rest by lying down outside of the restaurant. We wound up just like the people we saw when we first arrived. (By the way, that restaurant went out of business; it couldn't make money catering to people without self-control.)

All of us can lose our self-control; I, alas, am no exception.

To help define what self-control is, we play a simple game called Who Made You Move? In this game, first have children use their hands to follow the various movements of a Slinky as you open and close it. Next, ask the question that so affected me during my dance therapy class: "Who made you move? Was it me, was it the Slinky, or was it yourself?" Someone might say that you made him move. Point out that you didn't come over to him and move his hands for him; in fact, it would be impossible for the Slinky to come over and move his hands. All the kids made themselves move, and that's called self-control. Children learn that they must take ownership of their self-control and that only they can control themselves.

After you play the game, you can share stories about times when you have or haven't used your self-control. We've heard kids tell us about refusing to be drawn into confrontation, avoiding the temptation to insult or tease others, sharing with a friend instead of fighting, or getting their homework done rather than watching TV. Their eyes sparkle when they talk about these things; kids are proud when they realize that they have used self-control, and they want to tell you about it. They also want to hear about your experiences. You can share stories with them about times when you have or haven't used your self-control. In the process, children understand that you're not asking them to do anything that you, as an adult, don't have to do too.

I was driving in California once when another driver cut me off. I lost my self-control for a moment, honked, and made angry gestures. The other driver yelled at me, asking if I wanted a fight. In that moment, I realized that I needed to use my self-control to avoid turning an annoying situation into a dangerous one. In the nation that invented the term "road rage," a physical fight over a minor traffic infraction could easily turn deadly, and I realized that it was my responsibility to use self-control and defuse the situation. I simply drove on.

Sometimes I'm not using my self-control when I buy things impulsively. I once bought a treadmill and a pair of roller skates on the spur of the moment. It takes self-control actually to use these things for exercise, which I don't always do. Sometimes I use the treadmill just to get the dust off of it.

When ABC did a story on Lesson One, it showed footage of me walking through a classroom, in front of a line of kids, blowing bubbles. This is a great way to help teach kids an important notion. If somebody walks in front of your face blowing bubbles, whether you're young or old you're going to have a natural reaction: You're going to want to turn and follow the course of the bubbles through the air, and you're going to want to grab at the bubbles and burst them. That's simply human, and that's why we use bubbles as a teaching game. The children want to break the bubbles, or step on them, or simply look at them. Eventually, though, they use their self-control to stare straight ahead, unmoving. Although the bubbles are an enjoyable activity, there is a serious message involved in this game. The bubbles represent things that we shouldn't touch, such as guns, drugs, alcohol, cigarettes. This gives kids a concrete image of what to do or not to do and real-life experience in resisting tempting activities.

In the musical *West Side Story*, needless deaths occur because of a lack of impulse control. Gang wars rule a neighborhood, and teenage deaths are a gruesome result of vengeful rage and lack of

self-control. Two groups war against each other and think that
they are enemies because they belong to rival gangs. Really,
though, they are their own enemies because they lack self-control.

As kids begin to comprehend self-control, you can use that new
understanding to help them grasp important life lessons. Let
them know that they can use their self-control to refuse when
other kids want them to do dangerous things. Using self-control,
they can turn away from cigarettes and alcohol, they can refrain
from fighting, they can respect the property of others, and they
can stay away from guns and other weapons.

One guidance counselor told me a story about how his
Michigan school was threatened by a tornado. Using their self-
control, 360 children filed calmly into a hallway and hunkered
down, heads covered, for forty-five minutes. Their self-control
was so complete that it inspired calm and confidence among the
adults around them. "When the all-clear was finally sounded,"
Steve Hamilton recalled, "dozens of children came up to me to
tell me how they used self-control to keep themselves calm,
even though they felt scared, and how proud they were of themselves."

Self-control is necessary for any society to survive and succeed. It is vital that we all internalize this skill and pass it on to
our children. "If they don't understand how to use self-control in
the second grade," says Costella Laymon, one of the greatest
teachers I've worked with, "what are they going to be like in sev-
enth or eighth grade?"

The movie *The Day the Earth Stood Still* provides a chilling vision of what the world would be like without self-control. When
a flying saucer lands in Washington, D.C., the humans' first reaction is to shoot at it, thus wounding the humanoid alien piloting

the ship. They act on impulse because they feel threatened. They don't use their self-control and wait to find out what the alien wants. The alien realizes that Earth is a violent place, fraught with prejudice and pettiness. As a response, the alien shuts off all the electrical power on Earth for half an hour.

Rather than celebrate diversity, the first impulse of the humans is to shoot. Because of fear and frenzy, they could not accept this alien. The writer, Edmund North, and the director, Robert Wise, captured the bad side of human nature all too well. The film is a parable of how we will never have world peace until we learn self-control.

Wise, a warmhearted Indiana native, went on to make the classic musical *The Sound of Music.* In that film, Captain Von Trapp is a naval hero who deals with his children in rigid military style. He summons them with a whistle and identifies them each by an individual whistle sound. And while the children use extreme self-control to respond with military precision in their father's presence, they turn to mischief as soon as he is gone. They never internalize self-control. They spend their time terrorizing the long line of governesses the captain hires to take care of them. However, when Maria comes into the family, she puts an end to this behavior and helps them internalize self-control by relating to the children on a personal level, playing games, singing songs, and sharing stories. This relationship of mutual respect allows the children to be themselves and grow emotionally within the boundaries and structure of using self-control.

Self-control helps us naturally be ourselves rather than rigid and robotlike. Just like Maria, you can help children internalize self-control in a fun way by making it something that they can understand and use as a part of their lives. Adults might give children catch phrases, cues, or commands in the way that Captain

Von Trapp did. This can work. Children may be conditioned to learn to stop or to go when they hear a noise or see a color. However, this approach does not help kids take ownership of their actions and understand, internalize, and practice skills that they can apply for the rest of their lives.

When children learn how to use self-control, they learn how to be successful in our culture. Instead of allowing themselves to become victims of others or of their own negative feelings, they understand that they are the only people who can control themselves. This lesson can save lives. From random acts of violence to war, lack of self-control is at the root of much human suffering.

At a school in Connecticut, a kindergarten student became violent one day. It took several adults to restrain him; he even head-butted the principal and left a black-and-blue mark on her chin. The child scared many of the other students during this episode. Sitting in the principal's office, he discovered the Slinky and some of the other materials we use to define some of the skills. He was reminded of his self-control. He started to calm down while playing with the Slinky. He then said to the principal, "I want to get my self-control back. I'm sorry."

Even though the child had lost his self-control, he had a point of reference for what it was. This child went back to the skill he had learned. He wanted the structure and consistency to put self-control back into his life so he could feel proud of himself. But what happens to all of those children who don't have the skills to go back to? They get more and more out of control, and they have nothing they can fall back on.

Using self-control can help a child succeed in school, an athlete train hard, a writer finish a book, a nation avoid a war. Self-control is necessary for survival. That's why it's one of the first skills we teach.

## Teaching the ABCs of Life:
### Self-Control

·····································································

## 1: *INTRODUCE AND DEFINE IT*

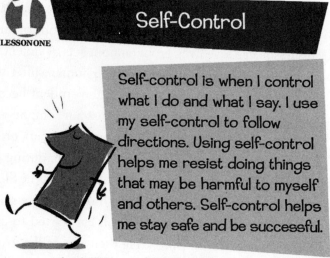

**Self-Control**

Self-control is when I control what I do and what I say. I use my self-control to follow directions. Using self-control helps me resist doing things that may be harmful to myself and others. Self-control helps me stay safe and be successful.

After cutting out the self-control poster in the Appendix, read the definition aloud together and introduce self-control. Here are some suggestions.

"We use our self-control when we take charge of what we do and what we say. We use our self-control to eat healthy snacks instead of junk food. When we get angry, instead of saying something mean that we might be sorry for later, we use self-control to keep our hands to ourselves, walk away from a dangerous situation, or talk about how we feel rather than pick a fight. Self-control is fun because we feel proud when we control ourselves.

When we don't use our self-control, we can become out of control and do things that we're not proud of.

"When we use our self-control, we can resist (or not do) things that may be harmful to ourselves or others. We use our self-control to stay away from things that may hurt us, like guns or drugs, and to stay safe. Whenever we use our self-control, we feel proud of ourselves."

## 2: EXPERIENCE IT
### Who Made You Move?

Has anyone ever asked you to do something that you'd gladly do, if only you knew how? This same thing happens to children when we expect them to use their self-control if they don't know what it is or how to use it. This game allows children to experience what self-control means and what it feels like to use it. Remember how much fun it was to play with a Slinky? Now we can use Slinky to help us learn self-control.

1. The only material you need for this game is a Slinky. Start by showing your children the Slinky and demonstrating the various ways it can move in your hands. Holding it on both ends, you can pull it apart, side to side, and up and down. You can jiggle the Slinky too.

2. Have your kids bring their hands in front of them with their palms facing each other. Give them the direction that when the Slinky opens up, they should open up their arms. When the Slinky closes, they should close their arms but try their best not to let their hands touch.

3. Once children have followed the simple movement of the Slinky, expand the game in various ways. You can make

the game challenging by moving the Slinky quickly and slowly while allowing it to change speed and direction. However, make sure the kids follow along as you lead the game. Jiggling the Slinky makes the game even more fun—children can shake their hands to correspond with the Slinky's movement.

4. Put the Slinky down and ask children, "Who made you move?" If they say that you made them move, ask if you came over and moved their arms for them. If they say that the Slinky made them move, ask if the Slinky came over to move their arms for them. Discuss the idea that they made themselves move. Then go on to explain that this is called self-control.

5. Now switch roles and ask a child to lead the game and move the Slinky while you use your self-control to follow its movement. This shows all the kids that adults need to use their self-control just as much as kids do.

FURTHER SUGGESTION

- You can have a lot of fun playing this game with a Hoberman Sphere. It is a multicolored plastic ball that expands and contracts when you pull on it or collapse it. Its colors and its unusual motion make it a favorite with kids.

After playing the game, discuss the following:

- Who controls what you do and what you say?
- Share examples of how you as an adult use self-control.

### Stop-and-Go Movement Game

We have all had to learn complex processes at some point in our lives, whether how to dance or how to drive or how to speak another language. When we learned how to do these things, we used a lot of self-control to follow the directions and to keep trying our best and not give up. Here's a game that gives children practice using their self-control without getting frustrated.

1. Gather a variety of instruments—and you can be creative about it. Radios, spoons, CDs, xylophones, rhythm sticks, drums, and noisemakers are all great materials to use in this game. After you've gathered these materials, tell the children that they're about to play a great game about using their self-control.

2. Give children a sneak preview of the game by allowing them to hear and see the noisemakers you have selected.

3. Choose a part of the body that children will shake when they hear the sound play. Children can shake their hands, head, elbows, knees, etc.

4. Go over the rules with the children. Tell them to shake the body part you've chosen when they hear the sounds you make. Tell them that when the sounds stop, they should use their self-control to stop moving and freeze until they hear the sound again.

5. Play the game. And while you're playing, please remember to be positive by telling the children what a great job they are doing using their self-control and that they should be proud of themselves.

6. Now give children a chance to lead the game while you play. Not only will they get to see you using your self-control, but they will also get to use the self-control it takes to lead the game and make sounds with the noise-maker.

FURTHER SUGGESTION

- Play the game again but change things around. Vary the speed of the game, or try a different body part. Pretend to make the noise but stop just before making it. Use two or more noisemakers and designate each one as a signal to move a different body part.

After playing the game, discuss the following:

- Who made you move?
- Whom should you feel proud of when you use your self-control?
- Discuss how you used the same self-control that it takes to listen and follow directions at home and school. For example, when I call you for dinner or the recess bell rings, you have to use your self-control to stop what you are doing and follow the directions.

## The Bubbles Challenge

Temptation is everywhere, and everyone gives in to it from time to time. Sometimes, though, these temptations can be dangerous. This game teaches children that they can resist temptation by using their self-control. When children avoid touching the bubbles, they are using the same self-control it takes to resist the dangers of alcohol, cigarettes, drugs, and guns.

1. Start by telling the children that you have a game for them that will challenge them to use their self-control.
2. Tell the children that you are going to blow some bubbles in front of them, and they have to use their self-control not to touch, step on, or even follow the path that the bubbles take as they float by their eyes.

3. Ask the children to stand so that they are facing a specific spot. You might want to give younger children an object that they can focus on in order to help them concentrate, such as a clock on the wall, a painting, or a piece of furniture.

4. Stand next to the children and blow the bubbles so that they pass in front of the children. Have fun with this; blow lots of bubbles so that they are close enough for the children to touch.

5. Remind children to keep using their self-control to not look at or touch the bubbles. Be positive. Tell the children what a great job they are doing using their self-control. Remind them that it's all right to make a mistake as long as they are trying their best and learning from their mistakes.

6. Challenge the children to use their self-control even more. Ask them to blow bubbles in front of you. Not only will this show them that you need to use self-control to avoid temptation as they do, but it will also give them another opportunity to use their self-control while they blow the bubbles.

FURTHER SUGGESTION

- To further challenge kids in using their self-control, have them pop only a certain amount of bubbles. First, have them pop only one bubble. Then have them use their self-control to pop only two bubbles, then three, then four, and so on.

After playing the game, discuss the following:

- Ask children to name some other times they have used self-control to resist temptations. (not eating candy right before dinner, not cheating on a test, avoiding the urge to steal something, keeping their hands to themselves, coming home on time, not smoking cigarettes, or even not touching a gun)

- Have a discussion with your child about times you both have or have not used your self-control. How did using your self-control help you? What can you learn from the mistake of not using your self-control?

## 3: SHARE IT
### Share Stories About Self-Control

As you begin to think about sharing from your own life, here are some anecdotes that friends, colleagues, and people from around the country have shared with me. Please share these stories and your own stories about self-control, and ask kids to share their stories about self-control too.

A woman told me about a personal victory she achieved through her self-control. When she went on a diet, she admitted it took a lot of self-control to ignore the ice cream she had in the freezer and the hot fudge that she had in the fridge. And she also used her self-control to use the treadmill at her gym three times a week, and by doing this, she said that she gave herself the strength to continue using her self-control. After she had been on the diet for a few weeks, the woman said that she realized that she had gained a lot of pride because she'd been able to control herself more than she ever had before. Now, she is excited about finding out what else she can do by using her self-control.

Money and self-control are a problem, one man told me. No matter how old he is, or what life circumstances he faces, he says that he always finds an excuse not to save money. Sometimes he has jobs that don't pay too well, but even then he spends money frivolously. And now he is in his early thirties and is afraid that he won't be able to start a retirement savings plan or put away money for his daughter's college education. This is the time, he says, when he must learn some self-control when it comes to money and savings.

A fourth-grade girl told me that her family had recently connected its home computer to the Internet. She says that as soon as she comes home from school, she goes on the computer and talks to her friends, does research for homework assignments, and goes to the Web sites for some of her favorite sports teams. But she says that her parents remind her to be very careful, because it can be dangerous to go to online chat rooms and talk to strangers when there are no adults around. Sometimes, she says, the chat rooms sound like a lot of fun. Still, she uses her self-control to keep herself safe and stay away from these chat rooms when the adults aren't around.

A sixteen-year-old told me that he once spent a lot of time with friends who are older than he. The young men had been pressuring him to try drinking and smoking marijuana, and on some nights, he had come close to trying them, even though he didn't really want to. After this happened a couple of times, he stopped seeing these friends so often. He felt pressured by them and said that he used his self-control to keep his distance from them and the unhealthy things they kept offering him.

## Self-Control Discussion Starters

Communication is vital to any interactions between adults and kids. To make sure that your kids understand self-control, it's important to discuss it with them and listen to their insights. Here are some useful questions.

- How can using self-control help keep you safe? Discuss using self-control to keep your hands to yourself, follow directions, listen, walk away from bullies, and also avoid unhealthy behaviors such as smoking and drug and alcohol use. What would happen if you did not use self-control?

- How can using self-control help you do well in school? (You use your self-control while studying, following directions, or not talking to your neighbor.)

- How can using self-control help you get along with friends? What would happen if you did not use self-control with your friends?

- Think of a time you used your self-control in a difficult situation. How did it feel?

- Think of one area in which you need to improve using your self-control. Try your best to practice the skill. Together, check to see how you're doing. For example, your goal may be to use self-control to drink more water than soda, and the child's goal may be to use his or her self-control to share with a brother or sister.

## Skill Builders for Adults and Children

- Think of someone you recently saw or heard about who used self-control.

- Think of someone you recently saw or heard about who did not use self-control. What could the person have done differently?

- Think of a time in the last week when you used self-control.

- When did you not use self-control but wish you had? What could you have done differently?

- Have a conversation about role models—people you know—who use their self-control.

- The skills are everywhere. Give an example of a book, movie, current event, or television show where people or characters either used or didn't use self-control.

## Helpful Hints

The mass media show us many examples of how people use and don't use their self-control. The most successful shows on television nowadays tend to feature violence, greed, deception, and irresponsible personal behavior. You can't shield your kids from what's going on in the culture, but you can use these TV shows, movies, books, or news events as opportunities to teach self-control. If a child sees violence on a TV show, talk about how the criminal could have acted differently using self-control. If the news talks about corporate executives committing fraud or people robbing banks, talk to your child about how self-control could have helped them find other ways to behave. Even the villains in children's fairy tales can provide a great launching pad for discussion. And when specific situations crop up with friends or family members who did or didn't use self-control, turn them into life lessons by discussing how they relate to self-control.

You can use any of the self-control games in many different situations. For example, teachers can play the Bubbles Challenge before a field trip to help remind children how important it is to use self-control while outside of the school. Children will need to resist the temptation to wander off and to refrain from talking or fooling around while important directions are being given by chaperones and presenters. If you are a reading volunteer or mentor working with children, the Stop-and-Go Movement game is a fun way to remind children that although you are there to help them, it's up to the children to control themselves. You can then tell them to use their self-control to follow directions and listen while you are reading to them.

Help a child who is having problems using self-control by noticing and praising when he does use self-control. Remind your child of the concept by asking, "Who controls you?" Help the child learn by noting how he feels when he does use his self-control. Then talk to him about how he can learn from his mistake when he doesn't use self-control. Self-control is a life skill that we all need to define, practice, use, and internalize.

Use the analogy of a car to describe the feeling of self-control. When you are in a car that's in control, you feel safe, just as it feels safe when you are in control of yourself. When you are in a car that is skidding out of control, it feels scary when you are out of control.

To help kids internalize the skill, use the term "self-control" when you give a direction. Saying things like "Shh," "Be quiet," and "Stop that" might work on occasion. Still, this doesn't teach children a skill that they can apply to other aspects of their lives. They are only following commands and doing it for the adults. Instead, remind your child to use her self-control, using either your firm and fair voice or your limit-setting voice, depending on the situation. This will also help give her ownership; she is learning to get her self-control back for herself. Take time to discuss the situation so the child can learn from losing her self-control. When the child has regained her self-control, tell her in your animated voice that she should be proud of herself.

~ ~ ~

If I were a cynic, I'd say that nothing unusual happened in today's news. It included the story of two teenagers committing murder, reports of a suspected terrorist attack, a child-abuse case—nothing, unfortunately, that you can't expect to see or read about at least a few times more this week and next week and, until we learn the skills for life, for many years to come.

The world can go on this way, or it can change. We can have war, terrorism, and violence, or we can build a better culture together. It all starts with self-control; as you will read in the following chapters, other skills build on self-control. If we raise a generation that learns these skills—and learn them for ourselves—we will discover, as Shakespeare said, that "there is a better world." It is important for everyone to understand that self-control is not just productive and practical. It is also fun. The consequences of using it are far more enjoyable than the consequences of ignoring it.

After teaching a lesson about self-control, a classroom teacher in Florida pointed out that the term "self-control" actually occurs in the second verse of "America the Beautiful." Sitting atop Pikes Peak on a bright, sunny day, the Wellesley College professor Katharine Lee Bates was overwhelmed. "When I saw the view, I felt great joy," she wrote. The patriotic anthem she composed that day represented her vision for her country's future, and she recognized that we would prosper as a democracy only if we embraced skills like self-control. The phrase "Confirm thy soul in self-control" reminds us that this skill is positive and majestic. It also underscores the importance of making self-control an integral part of our everyday lives.

# 6

# Self-Control Time

One visual image from the Lesson One program always amazes observers: the sight of children, some as young as prekindergarten age, calmly sitting with their eyes closed, looking proud and relaxed, slowly breathing in through their noses and out through their mouths. This is what we call Self-Control Time.

*Self-Control Time is a fun breathing exercise. It helps me calm down, focus, and get my self-control back.*

When we did a presentation at the White House, people were captivated by Self-Control Time. When ABC-TV and NBC-TV covered us, their producers had the same reaction. The *Parade* magazine article about us included a photograph of this remarkable exercise. Everyone was struck by how calm, centered, and attentive the kids in the classrooms were.

Anyone who has ever seen a typical kindergarten or early–elementary school class knows how chaotic such places can be. Sometimes children work in small clusters, which often erupt into loud talking; sometimes kids fight and often disrupt other students' work. Classrooms can become anarchic, with children frequently interrupting teachers and breaking into other kids' answers to questions or contributions to class discussions.

A little while ago, a friend of mine was asked to visit a second-grade class in an affluent New York suburb, to tell the children about his visit to Antarctica and the South Pole, a once-in-a-lifetime trip. He passed around his prized possession, a scrapbook of photographs of the Pole, penguins, the Antarctic ice, and glaciers. The class started getting out of control, and two adults had to take the scrapbook out of the hands of the kids, who were grabbing at it and came close to tearing these rare images into shreds. He realized that the lack of self-control is a near-universal epidemic, no respecter of socioeconomic situation, whether affluence, middle-class, or poverty; no matter what the setting, whether urban, suburban, or rural.

Schools simply reflect the culture in which we live; many children seem out of control, some of them violently so. But our society too often reacts to the problem by using external punishments or teaching through fear. On any given day in many schools, on the subway, or in the shopping mall, you're likely to see a frustated adult screaming at a fidgety, complaining child. Of course, publicly humiliating or, worse, physically punishing a child simply causes the cycle of rage and aggression to ratchet upward, out of control. People who choose these methods may eventually intimidate a child into submission for a while, but they will never teach the self-control every child needs as a skill for life.

When I was in elementary school, many teachers tried their best, but they perpetuated the dysfunctional ways in which they were treated as kids; they knew no better ways. My friend Annette Gromfin, an educational consultant, often talked about how assigning blame is counterproductive. She helped me understand that people just repeated the patterns they knew:

everything from students being sent to stand in the hallway to being hit with rulers. Teachers in the classrooms I have visited all over the country describe times from their own childhoods when teachers taped students' mouths shut, made them stand in garbage cans, and even placed dunce caps on their heads. Their teachers were frustrated, and so, out of fear, memory of what their own teachers had done, or hopelessness, they dealt with students in the only ways they knew.

One teacher remembered a time when, as a student, a teacher kicked her and pulled her down the stairs by her hair. Ironically, she ended up working in a school where that teacher had become principal. When we had a meeting with the faculty and staff before beginning a Lesson One program, the principal said that back then, she didn't know any better because that's the way she was taught to deal with children who acted out. She went on to explain that even in this day and age, she's concerned about how teachers are being trained and that's why she had invited Lesson One to her school.

Some teachers deal with a loss of self-control by giving their students extra work. And chances are that children who are punished with extra work in any given subject—copying definitions from the dictionary, doing a report, or doing extra math problems—will grow to dislike or resent that subject. When I was in school, teachers punished us by giving us "cubes." Anyone who had a cube had to come to school on a Saturday and do multiplication tables with a teacher. First, the teacher asked us a multiplication problem. When we got that right, we had to multiply this number exponentially—hence the word "cubes." The teacher stood above us and told us whether we were right or wrong. If we were right, she gave us another problem. If we were wrong, we had to keep on working. If we could not come up with the right answer by the end of the day, we had to come back the following Saturday. After a few Saturdays of cubes, I grew to resent math.

Such punishments are not just a thing of the past. A recent news story described the frustration of the mother of a middle school–aged son. She had spent years trying to get him to do his homework, but no matter what she did, he resisted. One day, she reached the end of her rope and ordered him to stand on a street corner with a sign around his neck that said, "I didn't do my homework." The sign also urged other people to honk their car horns if they agreed with the punishment. Police found the boy crying at an intersection, while other children walked by and picked on him. His mother defended her desperate actions by saying that she loved her son very much and wanted to steer him away from being irresponsible.

What kind of feelings must she have had while she drew the letters on that sign, while she sent him out to the corner, while she saw the tears and hurt in his eyes? It's not that this woman didn't care about her son. It's not that she wanted to hurt him. She just didn't know what else to do with him. We do what we are taught and what we see; she needed the ABCs of Life as much as her son did.

What did all of the corporal punishment and ridicule accomplish? Well, many of the stories we have heard came not from children but from adults, who remembered watching or suffering these indignities twenty or thirty or forty years ago. They still carry the scars. Perhaps, at the time, they modified their behavior to make the pain stop. But what good did it do?

I knew, almost from the minute I started Lesson One, that I had to find a way to help children learn a way to calm down and regain self-control that would not humiliate them, traumatize them, or, worst of all, physically injure them. When a child is punished this way, something is always taken away: self-respect, responsibility, even trust in the adults in the child's life.

Again, the point of telling these stories is not to assign blame. The point is to illustrate the fact that people sometimes repeat what they have seen. They repeat what's happened to them. Pointless, counterproductive punishments have occurred throughout history. In colonial times, almost every schoolteacher kept a birch switch handy and used it to whip students who wouldn't behave. Students who were caught talking in class wore wooden "whispering sticks" in their mouths. If students were caught biting their nails, they wore a card that said, "Bitefinger Baby." Students who didn't pay attention to the schoolmaster had to wear signs that said, "Idle Boy." I'm not pointing fingers; some people try their best, but they just don't know what to do. This is reality. Punishments like these have been a part of our culture for centuries. Some parents hit children because that's how they were raised; some teachers embarrass students because that's what happened to them or those around them.

When the late Thurgood Marshall, the lawyer who helped bring about the desegregation of America's schools and later became the first African American Supreme Court justice, retired from the Court, he held a rare press conference to announce his decision to leave. His health was clearly failing; he didn't live much longer. Someone asked him what he wanted written on his tombstone. He answered simply, "He did the best he could with what he had."

That's all any of us can do—the best we can with what we have.

Think about what we now consider some of the more humane ways of dealing with children who act out. Take time-out, for instance. When parents punish a child by giving him or her a time-out, or when teachers give children more work in a certain subject, they are not helping these children internally. It's not that these practices don't work—they can. However, time-out happens after the fact. It singles out a child after he or she has done something wrong, or hasn't done something that he or she should have done. It doesn't teach a child how to regain his self-control. It's not preventative because it doesn't prompt a child to take ownership of his or her actions. Often, time-outs become a pattern; children act out so that they will get the attention of an adult. The fact is that if you don't know what self-control is, you won't be able to get it back.

Adults and children alike talk of being stressed by the demands and challenges of jobs, schools, families, and activities of daily life. It's easy to become overwhelmed. We all hold stress and tension in our bodies. Research shows that young children are now experiencing anxiety attacks. Stress has the potential to cause a variety of physical ailments, including high blood pressure and heart attacks; it has been linked to a rise in suicide rates. Some experts have even theorized that it may be implicated in cancer and other diseases. Stress touches everyone; this is a fact that must not be overlooked.

How can we learn to reduce stress in our lives and the lives of children? How can we keep ourselves safe? How can we calm down and get our self-control back?

In response to all of these questions, Lesson One created the practice of Self-Control Time, a simple and fun breathing exercise. We've already covered the skill of self-control, and it's important to address the fact that we all lose our self-control sometimes. It's natural. Self-Control Time helps us understand how to get back self-control if we feel as if we are about to lose it or have already lost it. When we feel angry, upset, or excited, Self-Control Time is an internal tool that we can use to help ourselves. It's okay to feel a variety of emotions, but it's not okay to take these feelings out on others by hurting them or yelling at them. Most important, Self-Control Time is a concrete, positive tool that gives us the energy to deal with life and all of its twists and turns. Self-Control Time is a way of caring for yourself. It's a way for kids and adults to be proactive so that they can be ready to face the challenges that life brings. It's a natural antidote to stress.

Self-Control Time helps its participants to untie the knots—both physical and mental—that daily life creates. With their backs against the backs of the chairs, their feet flat on the floor, their eyes gently closed, and their shoulders relaxed, they can breathe deeply and bring air into their lungs and oxygen into their bloodstream. As they breathe in, they send oxygen through their lungs and into their brain, which helps them to think more clearly. Their heart rate slows, and they become focused and centered.

Self-Control Time is not meant to single out any individual. Although you may ask a child who has acted inappropriately to take a Self-Control Time, it's important to reinforce the idea that Self-Control Time is something that benefits us all. It should be a regular part of the school day and of life at home as well. Adults should talk about how they do Self-Control Time, to bring home the message that it's not a punishment but a positive way to help us make the transition from one activity to another, to focus, and to relate well to others. If children are playing sports, remind them that they have to exercise and practice before they actually play the game, whether it's field hockey or football. Self-Control Time is an exercise as well. Families, clubs, and other groups of people can use it—from children on school buses to adults in their offices or on factory floors.

Self-Control Time is not a meditation or a religious practice—it's natural. Too often, our bodies are tied up in knots because of the skyrocketing stress levels we all live with these days. We cross our arms, tense our shoulders, cross our legs. When adults are stuck in traffic, they often grip the steering wheel and hunch their bodies forward. That's not going to help them get to their destination any faster. It's unnatural *not* to do Self-Control Time. When we breathe heavily and our muscles are tight, whether it's after recess or playing a sport or a long day at work, we are not allowing ourselves to get back our self-control, to relax and be ready to control our days and our lives.

The practice of Self-Control Time began during Lesson One's infancy. Two kids from two different neighborhoods and cultures began to argue. It was obvious that the situation would escalate to a physical fight: One was preparing to use karate on the other. We told them to go back to their seats, close their eyes, and take a breath, and Self-Control Time was born. Initially, though, we called it Relaxation.

At first, children did Relaxation individually, after they became overexcited or did something inappropriate. We soon realized that this practice made children feel too isolated. Like time-out, it took place after the fact. But we discovered that some children were acting out because they wanted to get a chance to relax. We rethought the process and started doing it on a regular schedule with whole classes, in addition to using it with individual kids when they needed it. We chose times when children naturally needed to calm down, like after lunch and after recess. We learned that it needed to become proactive, to allow children to take ownership of their actions. It was a time when children could get back their self-control. We renamed it Self-Control Time and explained that this is not merely a rest period but an actual opportunity for refocusing one's energy.

You can use Self-Control Time to help children stay focused and calm throughout their day. We have found that Self-Control Time works best if a child does it for approximately three minutes, whether at home or in school. You can designate natural transition times in your child's day for Self-Control Time.

In school, teachers find it most effective to do Self-Control Time two or three times throughout the day. At home, find the best time to do Self-Control Time for each individual child. The point is to make it natural. For example, in the classroom, students begin their days with a Self-Control Time. We tend to assume that the students' days start when they get to school. But that's not true. Just like adults, children have to wake up, get dressed, eat breakfast, and get ready for the day by packing their backpacks. They might spend time playing with or taking care of a family member. By the time some students get to school, they feel as if they've already had a whole strenuous day. When they get to school, they should take about three minutes to sit down, relax, and focus. This can happen at home, as well. Before leaving for school, children can sit down and do Self-Control Time on their own to prepare themselves to start the day.

We ask students to do another Self-Control Time after lunch or after recess. These are times after which students need some winding down. Too often, students rush from one subject to the next, while they are still mentally out on the playground. We ask them to do Self-Control Time so that they can regain their focus and be able to try their best in the next class. At home, this same principle applies. Self-Control Time can come in handy after playing a video game, after a friend leaves, after playing outside, or before doing homework.

Self-Control Time is also helpful at the end of the day, so that children are relaxed and centered and mentally prepared to get home safely. Many children don't go home after school—they go to day care, a babysitter, lessons, or sports. They need their self-control to take care of themselves when they are on their own, going to and coming from these activities. Once again, the same principle applies at home. Children can take Self-Control Time to calm down and focus after returning from a party, before or after playing a sport, or before going to bed.

By doing Self-Control Time two to three times per day—in the morning, at midday, and at the end of the day—it soon becomes a natural part of a child's life. What additional times work for you? After you get home from work in the evening? During an argument? After exercising? Children might also do Self-Control Time when they can't fall asleep, when they are angry at a brother or sister, when they need to focus for a task. Adults and kids have countless opportunities for Self-Control Time. Even at the beach, Self-Control Time is a great way to relax. Use it as a way of putting your needs first while also preparing yourself to deal calmly with others.

How can children use Self-Control Time to help them regain their self-control once they have already lost it? In this case, a child can do a quick Self-Control Time for approximately one minute. For example, if your child is fooling around in a restaurant, and you can tell that she is about to lose her self-control, or if children are about to play a game of checkers and they begin to argue over who gets to go first, then you can ask them to do Self-Control Time.

First, use your limit-setting voice and, right where the child is sitting, ask her to close her eyes and take a Self-Control Time. Then, have her breathe deeply, for approximately one minute, and calm down to regain her self-control. Next, in a calm way, ask her to open her eyes. In your firm and fair voice, ask a question that will help to ensure that she takes ownership for losing her control. For example, you can say: "Who has to control you?" After the child is using her self-control, use an animated voice to let her know that she did a great job getting her self-control back and should be proud of herself. Self-Control Time is not a punishment. It is an opportunity for children to calm down and regain their self-control in a positive, nonthreatening way.

By using Self-Control Time, you can prevent a situation from escalating. After children have regained their self-control, you can talk about how we all lose our self-control sometimes, but it is up to us to use Self-Control Time to get our self-control back. You might even give an example of a time when you lost your temper and needed to do a Self-Control Time to help calm yourself down. When you use Self-Control Time with your children, you will be able to provide them with the structure to help them get their self-control back.

Does it work? A teacher named Jonathan Heller told me the story of a student on the soccer team he coached. The team reached a regional tournament, and the boy grew nervous as the first game approached. Before the game started, he sat down on the bench and took a Self-Control Time to calm himself down. Heller says, "The other kids didn't know what he was doing—but he played an outstanding game." Because the boy was relaxed, calm, and focused, he was able to try his best as he played. Other children took note of what a transformation had taken place. "By the end of the tournament, everyone was doing it," the teacher reports. That's the kind of effect that Self-Control Time can have: The kids were excited to learn a way to help themselves.

A second-grade girl in Boston told me about a time when she was visiting her grandfather. He had suffered a heart attack and was still in the early stages of recovery. While they were walking up the stairs, he ran out of breath, and the little girl started to get nervous. So she suggested that both she and her grandfather sit right down on the stairs and take a Self-Control Time. After they were done, they continued going up the stairs. Now her grandfather uses Self-Control Time as a regular part of his day.

When my sixth-grade teacher used to daydream during class, her mouth would hang wide open. The boy who sat behind me used to make mooing noises, which would crack me up. Although I knew he was being disrespectful, I couldn't help laughing out of silliness. When this happened, she would send me to the principal. To keep from getting in trouble, I asked to see the pictures that the principal had taken of his world travels. One time, I asked to see the pictures of his trip to Egypt. I told him that I wanted to know what the backside of the sphinx looked like, which I found hilarious. Rather than punish me, the principal invited me to come back the next day to have tea and look at the slides. I used a lot of creativity to stay out of trouble. All of this could have been avoided if I had known how to take a Self-Control Time. If I had been able to get back my self-control and calm myself down, I could have channeled my creativity more appropriately.

Kids who have the benefit of learning Self-Control Time have much more positive experiences. Once, after I taught a class about Self-Control Time, a boy told me a story about how he had been waiting to play with his friend's video game, but his friend refused to give it up. He admitted that he was tempted to hit his friend and grab the game away from him, so he went outside and did a Self-Control Time. After he was done, he came back inside, and he and his friend talked about how they could solve their problem.

One parent, Beverly Dunne, told us a story about a time when she and her husband took their five-year-old daughter to a hospital because she had developed a strange bump on her arm. When the anxious mom and dad were told that the girl needed an MRI, the physician explained that they do MRIs on children that young only if they are anesthetized. If you've ever had an MRI, you'll understand why: The loud clanking noises, the claustrophobic tunnel, the seemingly endless time it takes to do the procedure make most adults uncomfortable. For anyone, the experience can be terrifying. However, the use of anesthesia would delay the results. The physicians were skeptical that the young girl could lie absolutely still for forty-five minutes in the MRI tube and asked the parents if it was possible.

"Of course," they said. Their daughter had studied Self-Control Time at school and she knew how to use it. Her parents reminded her to do a Self-Control Time if she needed it during the procedure, and she did. She got through the MRI without moving and without anesthesia. The doctors and nurses were amazed. They had never seen anyone so young stay so calm while getting an MRI. They saw Self-Control Time in action. The little girl came out just fine, and the bump on her arm went away after a few months.

As a culture, we need to slow down and unwind. But in an era of multitasking, slowing down is too often viewed as lazy rather than necessary. Exhausted people complain of being pulled in a million different directions. The pressures are especially hard on children, who are often heavily scheduled with extracurricular activities and classes. The stress can take its toll on children and families alike.

Doing a Self-Control Time is like taking a quick nap. For some people, this might be the only time that they experience a quiet moment throughout the day. It opens us up to a new reserve of energy and gives us a fresher perspective on the day. It puts us ahead of what happens. Instead of responding to things in a frenzied and harried state, we are able to take the opportunity to calm down and use our self-control to try to make things happen the way we want them to happen. This holds true for adults as well as kids.

## Teaching the ABCs of Life: Self-Control Time

### 1: *INTRODUCE AND DEFINE IT*

LESSON ONE

Self-Control Time

Self-Control Time is a fun breathing exercise.

It helps me calm down, focus, and get my self-control back.

After cutting out the Self-Control Time poster in the Appendix, read the definition aloud together and introduce Self-Control Time. Here are some suggestions.

"In the past, people used to ask us to use our self-control without explaining what it was or who it was up to to use it. In many cases, people thought that the best way to help children get back their self-control was to have them wear embarrassing dunce caps, have them stand in corners, or even hit them with rulers. These people were trying their best, but they didn't know any better, because some of these things had been done to them too. When these things happened, children learned through fear, nervousness, or embarrassment. Now adults and kids can learn new ways to help themselves with self-control. Together, we can learn a fun and exciting way to help us get our self-control back. It's called Self-Control Time. Let's look at the poster to see what Self-Control Time looks like. Self-Control Time is a simple breathing exercise that gives us an opportunity to calm down, refocus, and get our self-control back. We can do Self-Control Time when we want to focus, when we play a sport or paint a picture, when we want to calm down before doing gymnastics, or when we do our homework, or to help us get ready for an exciting day. Let's go through the how-to guide together and learn how to do Self-Control Time."

It's important to remember that Self-Control Time is different from self-control. Self-Control Time is the breathing exercise that helps us get our self-control back. When asking a child to go into Self-Control Time, it's important not to call it self-control; that can cause confusion between the two skills.

## 2: *EXPERIENCE IT*
### Self-Control Time: A How-To Guide

Self-Control Time is an opportunity to help us calm down, relax, focus, and get back our self-control in a fun and positive way. We outline the Self-Control Time process here so that you can introduce this calming technique to your child. Please explain and discuss each section with your child.

1. **Self-Control Time is always done sitting down.** It is preferable to do Self-Control Time in a chair, because a chair provides structure. But you can easily do Self-Control Time on the couch, on the floor, on your bed, or at the park. It should be done wherever you are; no one should ever be sent to another room to do Self-Control Time, because it is not a punishment. It is a fun way to get your self-control back.

2. **Explain that we sit a certain way during Self-Control Time so that we can relax our muscles.** We sit in a comfortable way with our arms and legs uncrossed to help our muscles relax. This also helps oxygen flow through our body. Ask the children to cross their arms and legs and show them how bodies cannot relax when our muscles are tight and tense. Give them this simple example: When a rope is in a knot, it is tight. We don't want to make our bodies tight like knots. It takes a lot of energy to keep our muscles tight. We have to remind ourselves to let our muscles relax. To help children understand this, hold up your hands and have your children hold up their hands too. Make a fist. Ask them what they think is happening to the muscles in your

hands—are they tight or relaxed? Then ask everyone to open his or her fists, and explain that all of our muscles open up like this during Self-Control Time.

3. **Show children how to do Self-Control Time.** First, show children the picture of the boy doing Self-Control Time in the poster. If there are any questions, you can refer back to it to help clarify how to do Self-Control Time. Second, have children sit up, proud and relaxed, with their back against their chairs so that they are comfortable and the chair supports their back. Third, have children position their heads so that they are in a neutral position that faces forward rather than in a position in which the neck is bent back or hanging down. Fourth, make sure that their feet are flat on the floor. If they don't reach, they should just hang without being crossed. Fifth, children should straighten their fingers and put their palms facedown on their lap. Their elbows should be at their side. Discuss how, much of the time, we hold tension in our shoulders, hands, or other parts of our bodies. Notice where children are holding tensions and help them relax their muscles. For example, to help them relax their shoulders, you might ask children to lower their shoulders like an elevator traveling to the bottom floor. Finally, have children lightly close their eyes as if their eyelids are resting on top of a cloud.

4. **Practice breathing deeply while sitting in the Self-Control Time position.** Tell children that you are going to bring your hands in front of you and slowly open and close them like a slow, silent clap so that they can practice breathing. When you open your hands, children should breathe in through their noses. When you close your

hands, they should breathe out through their mouths. Explain that breathing deeply helps their heart rate (or the beats of their heart) slow down. Discuss how this will help them calm down, focus, and collect their self-control.

5. **Ask children to go into Self-Control Time.** Tell children that Self-Control Time lasts for about three minutes, during which they should remember to continue breathing in through their nose and out through their mouth. In a quiet voice, ask children to close their eyes to help them focus and relax. If necessary, remind them that you'll always be in the room while they do Self-Control Time.

6. **Help children stay in Self-Control Time.** In a positive way, check to make sure that shoulders are relaxed, feet are flat on the floor, hands are flat on laps, elbows are by children's sides, bodies are sitting up proud and relaxed with backs against the backs of chairs, breathing is deep, and eyes are closed. You can quietly give children reminders or give some positive reinforcements—let them know they are doing a great job!

7. **After about three minutes, have children open their eyes.** To help keep a calm environment, calmly ask children to open their eyes. Explain that they are now calm, relaxed, focused, and using their self-control. Tell children what a great Self-Control Time they just had.

FURTHER SUGGESTIONS

- Self-Control Time can also be done while sitting on the floor, if necessary. In this case, children should cross their legs and place their hands on their laps.
- On most occasions we found it effective to have children do Self-Control Time on their own while you help them—

checking that their shoulders are relaxed and their eyes are closed. Let children know that you do Self-Control Time when you need to focus and get your self-control back as well. Once kids have internalized Self-Control Time, there might be occasions for you and children to do it together.

- Have children show a relative, neighbor, or friend how to do Self-Control Time. The children can explain how it is done and why Self-Control Time is an important part of the day.

After practicing Self-Control Time, discuss the following:

- How does Self-Control Time help us?
- Talk with your child about occasions when you, as an adult, could do Self-Control Time. Ask him about times that he needs to regain self-control, calm down, or focus. These are times he could do Self-Control Time.

## 3: SHARE IT
### Share Stories About Self-Control Time

As you begin to think about sharing from your own life, here are some anecdotes that friends, colleagues, and people from around the country have shared with me. Please share these stories and your own stories about Self-Control Time, and ask kids to share their stories about Self-Control Time too.

During a family workshop, a grandmother raised her hand to tell a story. After she had retired, the woman joined a theater troupe in her town. On opening night of her first play, she was excited, but she was also very nervous. She even started to forget her lines. But then she remembered something her grandson had

# HOW TO DO SELF-CONTROL TIME

* Sit up proud and relaxed wherever you may be (a couch, the floor, a chair, etc.).

* Place your feet flat on the floor in front of you. (If your feet don't reach the floor, your legs should just hang without being crossed.)

* Extend your hands palms down and place them gently in your lap. Make sure your elbows are naturally back by your sides.

* Relax your shoulders so the muscles around them are neither tight nor tense.

* Breathe deeply in through your nose and exhale through your mouth to help your body relax into this position.

* Close your eyelids lightly and continue breathing deeply.

* When using Self-Control Time as a regular part of the day, it should last approximately three minutes. When using it as a way to help regain self-control, it should last approximately one minute.

For your convenience, you'll find a copy of the above guide in the Appendix. You can cut it out and use it as needed.

taught her: Self-Control Time. After taking three minutes to calm down, relax, refocus, and get her self-control back, the woman went out on stage and had a great show. Now, she says, she plans to use Self-Control Time every time she performs.

When I was teaching, one of the room parents told me about a time when she was driving to the grocery store with her children. The kids were both sitting in the backseat, and they started to tease each other. As the drive went on, the teasing turned into a loud argument. Just as the woman was about to put on her right-hand blinker so that she could pull over, the car grew quiet. She looked into the rearview mirror and saw that her children were sitting quietly with their hands on their laps and their eyes shut. When they opened their eyes a few minutes later, she asked them what they were doing, and they told her that they were taking a Self-Control Time to get their self-control back. The rest of the ride was relaxed and calm. The woman admitted that she learned a lesson from her children that day, and now she herself uses Self-Control Time if she feels as if she might say something that would hurt someone else.

A young boy at a school I visited told me about a time when he was playing pool with his friends in his parents' basement. They started arguing about the rules. None of them could agree on what kind of rules they wanted to use, because they all knew different ones. The argument got pretty loud, but while everyone else was still yelling, one of his friends walked over to the couch and started to do Self-Control Time. Pretty soon, all of the kids were doing Self-Control Time. After that, they talked about their problem and decided it would be fun to put all of their rules together and come up with their own version of the game.

A few years ago, a girl told me a story that I will never forget. She was the older sister of twin brothers, she said, shaking her head. It hadn't been easy for her. She reported that they constantly came into her room and went through her toys and made a mess of things. When she was nine and they were six, her parents gave her a bike she loved: It was baby blue with blue flowers. One day, she came home from school and decided to ride her new bike. But it wasn't in the garage where she'd left it. She started to get a funny feeling; she just knew that her brothers had taken her bike. Sure enough, they had done an experiment.

They had rolled her bike down the hill—with no one riding it—because they wanted to see how far it would go. And the bike had crashed into a pine tree.

The girl told me that when she found her bike, she was intensely angry. But instead of getting back at her brothers, she decided to do Self-Control Time. Later, her parents took her to the bike shop to get the bike fixed and told her how proud she should be for using her self-control. And when she was finished telling the story, I could tell that she was.

### Self-Control Time Discussion Starters

Make Self-Control Time come alive as you and your child discuss when it would work best in your lives. Here are some suggestions.

- How can Self-Control Time help you calm down when you are angry?
- Discuss how Self-Control Time is never a punishment but is a simple and fun breathing exercise that helps us use our self-control. Explain what a good feeling it is to be in control of yourself. Remind kids that if they lose their self-control and are asked to do Self-Control Time, it's only a positive way to help them get their self-control back.
- Discuss how adults and kids lose their self-control sometimes, but the important thing is to be able to regain control with Self-Control Time.
- How do we sit when we do Self-Control Time? What does it do for our muscles or the tension in our bodies?
- Discuss at least one time that Self-Control Time would be helpful to both you and the child in the next couple of days.

## Helpful Hints

The most important thing about teaching Self-Control Time is to remind kids that everybody—adults and children alike—has a regular need for it. Like brushing our teeth, or eating breakfast, Self-Control Time is an activity that we should include in our daily schedules, for our own benefit. This isn't an onerous duty, it's a skill children will need all their lives. Whether it be in the morning, afternoon, or toward the end of the day, Self-Control Time can be a natural part of a child's life.

If children are not using their self-control, remind them that they are not being punished or humiliated by being asked to do Self-Control Time. They are helping themselves by taking the opportunity to use this fun breathing exercise to help them get their self-control back. No one is judging them, and no one is ridiculing them. Self-Control Time is a way of helping children calm down and get their self-control back.

When you are working with young children, you may find that it takes a minute for them really to get into Self-Control Time. They need more help and reminders of how to do the breathing exercise.

During Self-Control Time, some kids—on rare occasions—have a difficult time sitting still, relaxing their muscles, or even keeping their eyes closed. In these instances, modify your expectations according to what the child can actually do. In adapting this for certain kids, however, make sure you're being consistent with your voice and body language, as kids are looking for structure. For example, if a child is opening his eyes and peeking, use your limit-setting voice to correct that behavior. If a child has trouble with her self-control, it is natural that she needs more help with Self-Control Time. Using the limit-setting voice pro-

# HOW TO HELP A CHILD REGAIN SELF-CONTROL WITH SELF-CONTROL TIME

* If a child is not using self-control, begin by reminding the child to use his or her self-control.

* If the child has not regained self-control, use your limit-setting voice and say, "Please take a Self-Control Time to get your self-control back." (Remember, the child can do Self-Control Time wherever he or she is—not in a special seat.)

* Remind the child that Self-Control Time is not a punishment, but an opportunity for the child to regain self-control.

* Have the child breathe deeply in through the nose and exhale through the mouth.

* In a firm and fair voice, calmly ask the child to open his or her eyes. Ask, "Who controls you?" Make sure the child realizes that it is up to him or her to use self-control.

* When the child is using self-control, remind the child to be proud of himself or herself for getting self-control back. Discuss with the child how Self-Control Time is a positive experience.

* This Self-Control Time lasts for approximately one minute. This differs from using Self-Control Time as a regular part of a child's day, when it lasts for approximately three minutes.

For your convenience, you'll find a copy of the above guide in the Appendix. You can cut it out and use it as needed.

vides the structure that will help them during Self-Control Time. When the child is using her self-control, go back with your animated voice and tell her something like, "Great job, you should be proud of yourself." As kids grow more comfortable with Self-Control Time, you can increase your expectations of what they can do.

During Self-Control Time, we ask children to sit up, feeling proud but still relaxed. When children cross their arms and legs, it's as if they're tying their bodies up in a knot. And just as a rope becomes tight when it is tied in a knot, children's bodies become tight when they're tied in a knot. When they sit up proud and relaxed, we ask children to untie that knot and relax their bodies. Feel free to ask children to sit up proud and relaxed throughout the day—it doesn't have to just be during Self-Control Time. You can ask them to do it at the dinner table, when they're on the school bus, when they're waiting their turn at a sporting event, before playing a musical instrument, or when they are working on an assignment for school. Any setting is appropriate for Self-Control Time. Children can take a Self-Control Time to help them calm down on a car trip or when they are waiting at the doctor's office. An instructor for children in after-school programs such as dance, swimming, or chorus can have children do Self-Control Time before instruction begins to help them transition from a busy day and focus on the task at hand.

Self-Control Time is a positive tool that can help you and your child focus, calm down, and stay in control so you can both do your best.

～　～　～

We live in a culture that is motivated by externals, including the ways we relax and deal with stress. When we want to calm down, we often do external things like overeat, or shop, or drink alcohol. Most of these things are fine when done in moderation, but they are dangerous when taken to the extreme. These coping techniques do not allow us to explore ourselves internally. We don't get to the root of what's going on in our lives. We don't figure out why we feel anxious or unsatisfied. We don't figure out what we need to do to satisfy ourselves.

Self-Control Time can catalyze a change in our culture. When we do Self-Control Time, we find a sense of focus that helps us feel refreshed internally and lasts longer than the quick fixes that material items, food, drink, and nicotine bring. Self-Control Time can be used consistently in any situation that requires us to center ourselves, calm ourselves, take on the day, and meet whatever challenges lay ahead.

In a culture beset with anxiety and anger, kids and adults instantly recognize Self-Control Time's power to calm and center them. They don't feel punished or put upon when they are asked to do Self-Control Time; far from it, they embrace it willingly, even joyfully. When it is properly taught, it is an exercise that people of all ages can turn to naturally in order to regroup, calm down, and focus. Self-Control Time can reenergize us.

As you read this, thousands of people from coast to coast are using Self-Control Time to center themselves and reclaim their lives. Imagine how much better society would be if every citizen used it to take control of his or her own life.

# 7

# Self-Confidence

When children make the Pledge for Success a part of their lives, use their self-control, and take Self-Control Time, they feel proud of themselves and begin to feel self-confident. We adults can watch and admire it, but it's not coming from us; externals have nothing to do with it. It comes from inside them. The whole point of Lesson One is to help kids and adults realize that the skills are internal, that their self-confidence comes from within themselves, and that self-confidence grows when they begin to use the skills and develop a proud, happy feeling.

*Self-confidence is a proud, happy feeling I get when I have tried my best. It's up to me to be proud of myself when I have done a good job. Some ways I show myself that I have self-confidence are by sitting, standing, and speaking with pride.*

Our country has been trying very sincerely and with great concern to address serious issues like school violence and drug abuse among young people. We've tried slogans like "Just Say No," and we've tried putting children on trial as adults. But those attempted solutions miss the point. They just repeat words or serve as punitive measures that are reactive rather than pro-active. They don't equip children with skills, and they especially don't address children's feeling of confidence. Kids who lack self-confidence are susceptible to peer pressure.

If you lack self-confidence, you worry that you won't be ac-cepted by whatever group you associate with—from a grade-school clique to a street gang to a country club. You feel that you have to do what they want you to. Rather than spending your time worrying about whether you fit in, you should remember that the most important thing is that you feel pride within your-self. With self-confidence, you are able to give yourself your own acceptance. Even if others criticize you, you find ways to see your own worth.

In illustrating the fact that self-confidence is not something that comes from externals, we talk about *The Wizard of Oz*. Think about the plot for a moment: Everybody in the film (per-haps excluding Toto) is looking for something external. They all think the wizard will give them a characteristic that actually comes only from inside: courage for the Lion, a heart for the Scarecrow, a brain for the Tin Man, and for Dorothy the ability to go home. In fact, the rock band America, in its most famous song, succinctly—if ungrammatically—captured the truth:

> . . . *Oz never did give nothing to the Tin Man*
> *That he didn't . . . already have*

Walt Disney's film *Dumbo* teaches us the same lesson. That lovable, whimsical story of the flying elephant demonstrates that externals aren't what give us self-confidence, or any of the ABCs of Life. Dumbo attributes his improbable ability to fly to a magic feather, but then one day, he loses it. What happens?

Nothing at all. He is startled to find that he can still fly. Nothing external gives him his skill; it comes from within himself.

The skill applies directly to our lives. We might work for a boss who praises us for doing a good job; we might not. Of course, it is preferable to work for someone who appreciates us, but what someone else does and says is not the most important thing. Whether it be at work or at play, we can't depend on others to praise us. If you're a plumber, a caregiver, a homeowner planting a garden, or an athlete playing a sport, you shouldn't expect constant external praise. What keeps us going is the self-confidence to be proud of ourselves and know that we've done a good job. Like adults, children often don't get praise for their efforts, whether they're trying something new, like an unfamiliar food, or they've made a new friend, or even when they try their best but miss a goal in soccer. It's up to us to tell ourselves when we have done a good job. A fire warden working alone in a forest observation tower, or a lighthouse keeper far from civilization may have nobody around to give constant praise and reassurance. People need self-confidence in order to feel proud of themselves and proud of the job they do.

In one of our workshops, a teacher confided that when she was a kid, she couldn't climb the rope in gym class. All the other kids made fun of her. Twenty years later, she walked back into the same gym class with the same gym teacher and climbed the rope. All the children in the class applauded. Although she had been belittled as a kid, at last, as an adult, she felt the confidence in herself to transform into a positive an experience that in her mind had been negative and hurtful. She realized that as a kid or an adult, you don't have to look for the applause but find it within yourself.

The late Ted Williams was the last .400 hitter in the history of baseball—a record that modern sports fans still look on with awe. But look at that record another way: It means that Williams failed to get a hit six times for every four times he got one. Did that keep him from being self-confident? Of course not. If he struck out, he waited his turn, came back to the plate, and tried again. He had self-confidence because he knew he was trying his best.

In a grade school in North Carolina, I asked a class to talk about how they used their self-confidence. One girl talked about walking away from a playground fight. That took self-control, of course, and self-control is a building block of self-confidence. And it was her self-confidence—her understanding that she was a worthwhile and good human being, that she could be courageous by ignoring bullies rather than by engaging them—that allowed her to avoid the fight.

In a similar situation, I heard a child making fun of another child during recess. To my happy amazement, this six-year-old child told the bully, "That doesn't bother me, because I'm my own engine." Powered by self-confidence, he simply walked away to play with other kids.

Bullies can take on different shapes and forms—some hurt with fists, while others use words as weapons. Whether they are adults or children, male or female, bullies lack self-confidence. They try to make themselves feel superior by targeting others. But this feeling doesn't last. And as soon as the insecure feeling returns, bullies look for new victims because the feeling of power over another is what they need to make themselves feel self-confident. But what happens when a bully doesn't have a victim? If the victim walks away from the bully with self-confidence, then the bully has no one to fight with but himself or herself. The only way that bullies can escape this pattern is to try their best and use their self-control so that they can feel self-confident.

It's important that children learn this skill early in life, so that they have practice with challenges that arise as they get older. Statistics show that children who begin smoking in their early teen years are far more likely to become lifelong smokers than those who never try cigarettes, or even those who just dabble with them in their late teens. The same is true of alcohol and illegal drugs. Many kids in late elementary, junior high, and early high school are at the greatest risk of succumbing to peer pressure. Self-confidence is a skill that, if they have acquired it early in their lives, enables them to walk away from such temptations. Other kids might call them names, but they know, with self-confidence, that they have done the right thing.

I see again and again the results of kids not having self-confidence. In New York, a group of young people went on a rampage in Central Park after a parade, assaulting and molesting a number of people. When they were arrested, many said that they had participated because their friends had pressured them to. In New Bedford, Massachusetts, a plot to stage a murderous rampage at the local high school was broken up only when police persuaded a teenage girl to tell them about the plans of the friends who had pressured her to join them.

It's not only kids who succumb to peer pressure. During the Watergate scandal, the country watched as men in positions of great power, one after another, confessed that they had, in Jeb Stuart Magruder's words, "lost their ethical compass." Under pressure to conform, John Dean, the White House lawyer; Charles Colson, a counselor to the president; and others knuckled under and participated in a criminal conspiracy. After they were released from prison, many of them began constructive lives, contributing to society by working with inmates and doing other good works. They are not congenitally bad people. But they lacked the self-confidence to walk away when others proposed that they do something wrong.

We all slip sometimes and let our self-confidence desert us. The important thing is to remember that self-confidence is a skill that stays with us for life. It's important to focus on the process of learning the skills, and if on occasion you don't use them, you can learn from your mistakes and try your best the next time.

When Mark graduated from medical school, mementoes of his medical career—everything from his graduation class picture to news clippings—decorated the walls of my father's office. When I started Lesson One, I received a lot of favorable attention from the press and public authorities. Whenever I visited my father, I hung some of the clippings and citations on his office wall. But by my next visit, they would all be taken down. This happened time and time again. Even though I knew that I was not going to get my parents' approval for the work I did—they had expected me to be a doctor, or at least a lawyer—I was still looking for it. But I realized, using a self-confidence that I had built up over time with help from Effie and others, that I didn't need their validation anymore. Any approval I needed would come from myself.

In our culture, in many cases, external beauty is of the utmost importance. In movies and magazines, women and men are glorified if they satisfy an almost unattainable standard of beauty. In our society, teenagers have begun requesting plastic surgery to "improve" their looks at younger and younger ages. They think that looking like their pop-star idols will help them to have self-confidence, instead of finding it from within. It's refreshing when a movie like *Shrek* shows that internal merit is more important than what's on the outside. By day, the movie's Princess Fiona is a gorgeous woman whose company is widely sought. As the result of a curse, though, Fiona changes into an ogre at night. She seals herself off from true love because she is afraid that others will find out that she is an ogre. At the end of the movie, though, she is changed into an ogre permanently, yet, at the same time, is accepted for who she is by the love of her life. The princess doesn't return to what our culture sees as beautiful but retains her own distinct inner beauty by being confident in herself.

We live in a culture of externals. When the former chairman of Enron left his job, his wife opened an entire store just to sell the expensive furnishings they had accumulated in their various homes. The former CEO of General Electric negotiated for a Boeing 737, an expensive Manhattan apartment, and a huge expense account as part of his retirement. This fixation on establishing your importance by the number of "toys" you have should come as no surprise. American advertising for years has been telling us that we need to buy the most expensive car, live in the most expensive house, take the most expensive vacations, own the most expensive designer clothes. You can't escape the commercialism in our culture. It's everywhere—on billboards, on flyers, on the Internet, in the mail, on coffee cups, on jeans and sweater labels. Every Saturday morning in children's television commercials, our kids hear that message as well. These things are supposed to make us feel good. How? You might feel good for that moment, but externals go away. What do you do when your clothes go out of style, or your electronics are outdated? It's important not to fall into the trap of basing our lives on what others tell us. You have yourself, and that is what you should base your life on.

Interestingly, when we go into classrooms and ask kids what advertisers are after when they push toys and shoes and games in their commercials on kids' shows, we get a surprisingly insightful reaction: "They want our money," kids tell us. We teach children about self-confidence to help them learn that no toy, no possession, no designer sneakers or trendy jacket, will make them better, smarter, or more valuable human beings. We are teaching the ABCs of Life, and in life, it's what's inside that counts. People feel good about themselves by trying their best and using their self-control.

When I was starting out as a teacher, I went to an in-service, a day when teachers leave the classroom to get together and share ideas about education. I was taken aback when I realized that the presenter was selling jars filled with toys to give out to kids when they performed well. He was telling us that these externals would build self-confidence. I was brash, young, and curious. I asked, "What happens when you run out of toys?" The presenter answered simply, "You buy more toys."

In front of all the other teachers, I announced that I thought the presenter was merely trying to sell us commercial stuff, not help kids. I suggested that children could better learn to feel self-confidence through themselves, rather than through getting external prompts and rewards. I didn't make any friends among the salespeople that day.

This is not to say that external rewards are always inappropriate; candy or toys can be used in a positive way as long as you and the children understand that they are transitional. The focus should be not on the toy or candy but on the fact that by doing a good job, they have earned the happy feeling of self-confidence for themselves. The aim is to wean children off these externals and teach them to do their best for themselves. With younger children especially, rewards can be effective in getting attention. But remember that your purpose is to help the child learn that self-confidence is internal. After all, what happens when the stamp wears out, the candy is gone, the toy is broken, or the sticker is lost? Does the child lose his or her self-confidence at that point?

When I volunteered at the Winthrop Nursery School, Hildred Simonds taught me how to wean children gently away from externals in a way that reinforced their understanding that their self-confidence, like all their skills, comes from inside them. A young boy was somewhat insecure. He brought to school some really cool toys, which the other kids envied and loved to play with. Mrs. Simonds sat down with him and learned, through her careful, patient listening, that the boy thought he needed to bring the toys so that the other kids would like him. She set up a plan, asking him every few days to bring fewer and fewer toys. Eventually he stopped bringing any at all and discovered that he didn't need the toys to get the kids to like him. Once he felt confident in himself, it was easier to make friends.

Right down the street from where I went to elementary school stood the world's greatest toy store. At least I thought so. I spent hours there during my lunchtimes and after school. My favorite toy was a trick camera. When you pressed the button to take a picture with the camera, a plastic worm shot out of the camera lens. I loved this camera so much that I used some of my lunch money to buy one. Everyone in my class loved it too, and I thought that as long as I had a camera, I would be popular. But these cameras were not well made, and mine broke. So I used more of my lunch money and bought another camera. They kept on breaking, and I kept on buying more. Then I saved up more money and bought a bigger toy, a marble maze. Eventually this broke too.

Having all of the things in the world doesn't make you happy. In *A Christmas Carol*, Ebenezer Scrooge learns that the single most important thing in life is human relationships. Even though my parents gave me things, what I really wanted was for them to show me love and affection. Even today, on occasion, when I experience highs or lows, I look for externals to make up for the love and affection that I didn't get early in my life. I eventually realize what I'm doing and reflect on what my real needs are.

The movie *Citizen Kane* is the story of a man who seemingly possesses most of the riches the world offers. Pauline Kael, who was widely regarded as the founder of modern-American film criticism, wrote an entire book about it; she thought it was the greatest film ever made, and many others agree with her. That's because it perfectly evokes some universal themes.

The film begins with Charles Foster Kane's childhood, as he gleefully plays in the snow with a group of friends on his sled, Rosebud. The movie quickly abandons this innocent focus as Kane's life starts to revolve around taking and getting money and power. As Kane dies a rich man, he whispers the word "Rosebud." At the end of his life, the internal joy of his childhood, not the external trappings of fame, wealth, and power, is what brings him happiness.

We teach the skills to children from prekindergarten on. Young kids are more open, more ready to understand, less likely to have formed negative ideas about their own self-worth. Orson Welles, when he wrote *Citizen Kane*, understood that Charles Foster Kane's most centered and internal moment came from his childhood. Younger kids can learn self-confidence easily.

That doesn't mean that older kids and adults can't. We all need to understand that we can feel proud of ourselves and can help instill self-confidence in others. Much of the time, we don't even realize that we are judging or labeling others.

An activity we play to help children reinforce and nourish their self-confidence is called Picture Yourself with Self-Confidence. Gather construction paper, crayons, and markers; if you like, add a few magazines. Also find photographs of the children (or have them draw self-portraits).

In this activity, children create a poster of themselves surrounded by pictures of hobbies, interests, and other things they enjoy doing that they are self-confident about. To begin, ask them to start thinking about those activities that make them proud and those at which they try their best. Next, have children place a picture of themselves on the construction paper and draw pictures (or cut out pictures from a magazine) that represent what they came up with.

We play this game to reinforce the idea that self-confidence is not about what's on the outside—it's about how you feel about the person you are on the inside. The goal is to create an "internal" picture, so that the children can visualize the qualities that help build self-confidence. When they are finished, have the children share with each other and with you what their pictures represent. Remind them to speak with self-confidence as they show their creations. Remind them that they should be proud of themselves.

"You're uncoordinated," the father of someone I know used to scream at him whenever he failed to catch a baseball or throw a football correctly. "Look at you; you'll never amount to anything; you can't even catch a ball. You never do anything right." (His father stopped saying those things around the time the son earned a degree with honors from Harvard. It's very sad that the father based his relationship with his son on external achievements.)

There are some grown-ups who think that upbraiding kids and pointing out their shortcomings is the best way to raise them. While self-confidence can come only from inside, its development can be hampered—and, in some cases, destroyed—by externals.

My high school's Latin teacher ran the school play every year. Each time, he gave out parts to his favorite students and ignored the rest of us. One day in class, I told him that I was trying my best, and he answered, "I know. I've seen your IQ scores, and you're only average." At the same school, I had a chemistry teacher who used to read our grades out loud; when he came to mine, he added a little aside, "You're the stupidest kid I ever met; this is the lowest grade I've ever given." Later, this same teacher accidentally set his sleeve aflame in a Bunsen burner. The fact is, we all make mistakes and have to try our best.

I had a friend who went to a very demanding secondary school; eventually, he did well and went on to Harvard, but his freshman year at the secondary school was a disaster. Faced with Latin, world history, algebra, English, and German, he got dismal grades in his first semester. At the end of the term, all of the students were called to the auditorium, where they were ordered to stand, one after another, as their grades were read off in front of the entire school. His were, like many of his classmates', low. Most of those first-semester freshmen skulked out, humiliated and depressed. Several dozen dropped out, although their aptitude tests showed they were clearly able to do the work.

"I don't know why we ever did that," one of his teachers confided at a reunion decades later. "It was sadistic."

The adults who decided to read every student's grades in

public thought that by shaming them they were motivating kids to do better the next time. They never realized that they were helping to destroy self-confidence, not enhancing it.

This is partly the reason cheating in school has become an epidemic in our society. The need to get a good grade because of the fear of failure, or the fear of disappointing our teachers or our parents, or the fear of embarrassment drives the desire to cheat. But in the end, if we cheat, we disappoint only ourselves. How can we be proud of ourselves if our accomplishments are obtained by subterfuge or illegal means? Self-confidence doesn't come from the externals of grades. Self-confidence comes from trying our best.

While self-confidence can come only from within, others can help plant the seed and help it grow. My English teacher, Dr. Kasendek, spent an entire class talking about my accomplishments.

Dr. Kasendek singled me out for attention and told the class that he had never seen any other student receive as much applause as I did when I made presentations or performed during assembly programs. He also threw in the observation that he didn't know any other kid who got along with as many people in all the other grades. Even as a kid, I always thought in an unconventional way. When we were supposed to write a paper on a great event in history, I wrote about "The Battle of Ants Hill." Dr. Kasendek frankly admitted that he had no idea what I would do professionally, but he told the whole class that I would always use my creativity.

One of my closest friends, John Higgins, influenced me greatly in showing me how a teacher can help inspire self-confidence in young people. Early in my career I taught creative dramatics at the elementary level; John was the high school dramatics teacher. When I went to the plays he directed, I was amazed that every kid who tried out got a part—sometimes John even rewrote plays to make sure that everyone got a place in the cast. Like an accompanist who transposes a piece of music to fit the vocal range of the singer, John made a point of adapting the script to the talents and needs of all his students. He put the kids first, because he understood that he was promoting their self-confidence and helping them learn an important skill.

Unfortunately, this isn't always a common practice. One parent told me about his son, who had a different style of learning from the other students in his classroom. All of the children were reading H. G. Wells's *War of the Worlds*—except his son. Instead, the teacher gave him a book that was appropriate for much younger children. He felt embarrassed and left out. Another friend, Arlene Shainker, a school psychologist, emphasizes that all books and materials can be adapted to all levels and abilities. In her work, she makes sure that no child feels inadequate due to his or her unique learning style.

A parent told me about her second-grade daughter, who had dyslexia and Attention Deficit Disorder (ADD). Her teachers didn't even put her in a reading group, unlike every other member of her class. When the young girl's class was asked to read to a kindergarten class, the teachers had a student from the kindergarten group read to the girl. She was humiliated. To help foster this child's self-confidence, her teachers should have given her something that she could do rather than embarrassing her and diminishing her confidence. It is imperative to look at everyone individually, regardless of the person's learning style.

These stories had a great impact on me. When I do activities, I make sure that everyone is involved. In typical games, someone might be left out. We never use games that exclude anyone.

Rather, we encourage all participants to keep on doing their best and learn from their mistakes. I learned how to make every experience as positive as possible for adults and children.

As adults, it's important that we support children in their efforts. However, so many times I've heard adults tell children how great they're doing and how wonderful they are even when the children are putting forth little effort. This does nothing to help with the skill of self-confidence; it only perpetuates the idea that they needn't try their best. Children will continue with this false self-praise throughout their lives.

Another game we play is Walk with Self-Confidence. The idea is to help kids internalize the idea of self-confidence by standing up for their own beliefs. As they play, they learn that self-confidence comes from themselves, not from other people or other things.

In this game, we ask a variety of questions to challenge everyone to stand up for what he or she believes in. For example, we ask everyone who likes to go skateboarding to move to one side of the room, and everyone who doesn't like skateboarding to go to the other side; people who haven't tried it or feel in the middle about it remain in the middle of the room. Instead of following what their friends think or being afraid to be standing alone, adults and kids stand at their destination with self-confidence. This is a good time to remind kids to stand up proud and relaxed, with their shoulders back and heads high.

This game builds on the Celebrating Diversity Game and is also a valuable and enjoyable way of teaching self-confidence. Remind the children to be honest, to respect one another's diversity, and, most important, to use self-confidence to stand up for themselves. This valuable game helps children use self-confidence later in life. If they are then asked to smoke cigarettes, or their friends aren't using their self-control in other ways, children will have a reference for using their confidence to stand up for what they believe in.

In the film *Twelve Angry Men*, Henry Fonda plays the only member of a jury with the courage to speak out and say that he believes a defendant is innocent. The movie exemplifies how important it is for people to have self-confidence and stand up for what they believe in. In the end, Fonda saves an innocent man from going to prison.

I've seen self-confidence work wonders in my own family. My son, Andy, wanted to take golf lessons a few years ago, so my wife, Mimi, and I signed him up for a week of golf day camp at our local community center. On the first day, they discovered that we had made a mistake and signed him up for the wrong week. He was in camp with the high school kids. Andy, nine years old at the time, said he wanted to spend the first day there to see how he'd do. The counselor agreed to let him borrow some clubs since we didn't have any. I spent the whole day biting my nails and worrying about how he was doing. To my pleasant surprise, when I picked him up, the counselor said that because Andy believed in himself so much, things went very well, and he could stay. When we got home, Andy explained to me with self-confidence how he "listened to their personalities, found out what they liked, they listened to me." As he put it, "I put it all in a blender and out came myself knowing what to do to get along with the other kids."

## Teaching the ABCs of Life:
## Self-Confidence

### 1: *INTRODUCE AND DEFINE IT*

**LESSON ONE**

## Self-Confidence

Self-confidence is a proud, happy feeling I get when I have tried my best. It's up to me to be proud of myself when I have done a good job. Some ways I show myself that I have self-confidence are by sitting, standing, and speaking with pride.

After cutting out the self-confidence poster in the Appendix, read the definition aloud together and introduce self-confidence. Here are some suggestions.

"Self-confidence is a proud, happy feeling we get when we try our best. We also feel self-confident when we use our self-control. When I did my presentation at work, I felt self-confident because I tried my best, just like when you performed in the piano recital and tried your best, you felt proud. I have to tell myself that I did a good job and that I should be proud of myself and feel self-confident, and you have to tell yourself that you did a good job and you should be proud of yourself and feel self-confidence. Sometimes, kids and adults think that we can get self-confidence from other things, like toys, cars, or clothes. But the feeling you get from these things is not self-confidence, because this feeling doesn't last. What happens when those things get old or break? Self-confidence comes from the inside. When you sit, stand, and speak with pride, you are showing yourself—and those around you—that you have self-confidence. To speak with self-confidence, first take a deep breath, then slowly begin to speak. This way not only are you speaking with pride, but others are also able to hear you. The only person who can give me self-confidence is myself, and the only person who can give you self-confidence is yourself."

## 2: *EXPERIENCE IT*
### Picture Yourself with Self-Confidence

When we picture ourselves with self-confidence, we should focus on who we are on the inside, rather than base our worth on the possessions we have. This activity illustrates this point by helping us reflect on interests, hobbies, and other things that we enjoy and try our best with.

1. Begin by collecting construction paper, markers, crayons, magazines, and a photograph of each child (or they can draw self-portraits).
2. Explain that the activity will help children understand what they should feel self-confident about.
3. Have the children place their picture in the middle of a large piece of construction paper.
4. Then discuss with the children things they can feel self-

confident about. Ask them to think of times when they try their best and they feel proud of themselves. You can help them come up with examples of self-confidence.

5. Next, have them draw some of their confidence examples surrounding their picture on the construction paper. Make sure that they don't choose possessions; they can choose hobbies, interests, activities, school subjects, etc. Children can also cut out pictures from magazines that represent ways they try their best and feel proud of themselves. For example, if tennis is something they try their best at, they can put a picture of a tennis ball or a racquet on their picture. In addition, children can add words, stickers, glitter, or any other decoration they feel helps represent their confidence.

6. You should create a picture too. This helps show the children that both adults and kids need self-confidence.

7. When everyone is done, hold up the pictures and have everyone talk about his or her creation.

8. Remind the children to tell themselves they should feel self-confident if they tried their best.

After this activity, discuss the following:

• Should you be proud of yourself even if you are different from your friends or classmates? How can you remind yourself of that?

• Is there something you like but are afraid to do? Should you not try it or use your self-confidence and just try your best?

## Walk with Self-Confidence

Sometimes it takes a lot of self-confidence to stand up for what you believe in, and we've all experienced how strong peer pressure can be. In this game, everyone in the room gets to express his or her unique feelings by relying on self-confidence.

1. Begin by explaining that everyone in the room will be playing a game that will challenge his or her self-confidence. They will have to use their self-confidence to be honest with themselves and stand up for what they believe in.

2. If you are playing with a large group, have the group stand up in a fairly open area of the room.

3. Ask everyone questions about likes and dislikes. (This is a variation of the Celebrating Diversity Game with an emphasis on self-confidence.) Begin by asking a concrete question to demonstrate how the game is played. For example, you can ask who likes to play basketball.

4. Explain that when you ask the questions, everyone who likes basketball can walk to one part of the room, while everyone who doesn't like basketball can walk to another part of the room, and those who feel in the middle about basketball or have never played basketball can walk to the middle of the room.

5. Remind children to walk with self-confidence and be proud of what they believe in. Also remind them to use their self-control to walk in an orderly manner, without making noise or disturbing others.

6. You can play too. By participating in the game, not only do you show how important it is for adults to have

confidence in themselves, but you also add to the climate of sharing by being open about using your self-confidence.

7. Once everyone understands the concept, be creative with your questions. You can ask about TV shows, foods, movies, places, toys, hobbies, etc. Avoid asking questions about people.

8. Remind children to be confident in their ideas and themselves. Self-confidence helps them to be honest, to celebrate diversity by treating others the way they would like to be treated, and to stand up for themselves and not follow their friends.

9. It is important to point out when only a few people stand on one side of the room. Compliment them on using their self-confidence to stand up for what they believe in, even if they are the only ones.

10. Tell the group that they should be proud of themselves for using their self-confidence by standing up for what they believe in.

11. Give the children who are playing a chance to ask the group the questions. You can provide them with categories for questions, like games, hobbies, or topics relating to a school subject. Make it clear that we treat others the way we would like to be treated; therefore, we don't ask about people. This is a great time for everyone to practice speaking with self-confidence too.

After playing the game, discuss the following:

- What skill did you have to use to stand up for what you believed in?
- How did it feel to use your self-confidence? Why?

- If your friends felt differently from you, could you still use your self-confidence to stand up for yourself? Was it easy? Discuss why it was easy or hard.
- When are some other times when we should all use our self-confidence to stand up for our beliefs?

## 3: SHARE IT
### Share Stories About Self-Confidence

As you begin to think about sharing from your own life, here are some anecdotes that friends, colleagues, and people from around the country have shared with me. Please share these stories and your own stories about self-confidence, and ask kids to share their stories about self-confidence too.

One of my friends talked about how it had always been his dream to take a scuba course. He wasn't much of a swimmer, and in order to enroll in a scuba class, he had to be able to swim two hundred yards. In fact, he had actually turned down someone who had asked him to take a scuba class with him. But then, a few years later, after taking a swimming course, he gave himself the self-confidence to try swimming the two hundred yards. He did it. He enrolled in the scuba course, and now he even has his scuba certification.

When a friend of mine was in fifth grade, her teacher told her that the reason she was having difficulty in math was that she was a girl. And she believed her teacher. Throughout junior high school and high school, she treated math with distaste: She never studied, she easily became frustrated, and she didn't ask for help because she thought that the situation was hopeless. But then in her junior year in high school, she had a math course with a very gifted teacher, who was female. My friend realized that she had let someone else's stereotypes and disregard for diversity affect her self-confidence. She went in for extra help when she needed it and actually studied for tests and quizzes, and, for the first time, she felt self-confident about her math ability and went on to take two calculus courses in college.

A girl told me a story about an assembly that had recently been held at her school. The members of her class were doing presentations on former presidents. The student who was playing John Adams got sick at the last minute and couldn't do his part. Everyone started worrying that the class wouldn't be able to do the presentation. But another boy volunteered to step in and play President Adams, even though he didn't know the lines. He stood on the stage while the teacher read the lines to him through the curtain; the audience didn't even notice. The girl said that the thing she really remembered from the play was how much self-confidence it took for him to do this.

When I was teaching a third-grade class, I noticed that a girl sitting in the front row was wearing a very colorful beaded bracelet. When I complimented her on it after class, she told me that she had made it. She had recently started making beaded jewelry, and usually, when she finished a piece, she immediately ran to show her parents what she had made so that they could tell her what a great job she had done. But the last time she had finished a necklace, she went to show it to her parents; they were busy talking to the neighbors. Then she looked down at the necklace and told herself that she did a great job. She realized that she didn't need her parents to tell her that she had done well, because she could tell herself.

## Self-Confidence Discussion Starters

Follow the games with discussions of how self-confidence works in everybody's daily life. Here are some questions you can use to get kids and adults talking.

- When you have done your best or used your self-control, who has to tell you that you've done a good job? (yourself) Discuss how you also have to feel self-confident at the end of the day even if no one tells you that you did a great job.
- When sitting, standing, and speaking with self-confidence, for whom are you doing that? (yourself) Why are sitting, standing, and speaking with self-confidence important for all of us?
- Name three reasons you feel confident about yourself.
- It takes self-confidence not to follow what your friends do and to be yourself. What are some times you can use self-confidence to stand up for yourself?
- When you are playing a sport or performing in a play and you try your best and make a mistake, should you still feel self-confident?
- Talk about the fact that we all like different things. Discuss how when we respect everyone's point of view, we are confident in ourselves.
- What is something new you can try with your self-confidence that you have always been nervous to do? Discuss how it's important for both adults and kids to use self-confidence to try new things. Together, choose one new thing to try.

## Skill Builders for Adults and Children

- Think of someone you recently saw or heard about who used self-confidence.
- Think of someone you recently saw or heard about who did not use self-confidence. What could the person have done differently?
- Think of a time in the last week when you used self-confidence.
- When did you not use self-confidence but wish you had? What could you have done differently?
- Have a conversation about role models—people you know who have self-confidence.
- The skills are everywhere. Give an example of a book, movie, current event, or television show where people or characters either had or didn't have self-confidence.

## Helpful Hints

Remind kids that it takes self-control and self-confidence not to follow what others do. It is important not to sound preachy, but discuss the fact that if a friend is not using self-control and smokes cigarettes, takes drugs, or steals, it is up to the individual child not to succumb to peer pressure and have the confidence to do what he or she knows is best.

As an adult, you often want to say to children, "I'm so proud of you." However, to help instill self-confidence, it's important that you first tell them that they should be proud of themselves. You can help children understand this idea by asking them to tell themselves something they did that day that they felt self-confident about. Begin by asking them to say this aloud. You won't always be there to remind children that they should feel proud, so to help them feel self-confident when they are on their own, have children practice silently telling themselves to be proud. That way, children will have the experience of telling themselves that they are proud of themselves and know what it is to feel self-confident. Children will be able to take this experience of giving themselves self-confidence and apply it when they're on their own.

Talk about how adults and kids all need to speak with self-confidence in order for people to hear what we have to say. What would happen if police officers, firefighters, teachers, actors, or salespeople didn't speak with self-confidence? Act out different voices—a shout, a timid voice, a self-confident voice—that these people could use.

If you cannot hear a child reading or speaking, ask her to speak up with self-confidence. Have the child take a breath before speaking to help her with self-confidence. Rather than slouching at their desks or in lines at school, students can sit and stand proud and relaxed with self-confidence.

You can naturally play the self-confidence games anywhere. The Walk with Self-Confidence game is fun to play at recess, children's birthday parties, family gatherings, drama lessons, sports practices, etc. It's an enjoyable way not only to help children with self-confidence but also to help everyone learn a life lesson while having a great time.

Society will be a better place if we raise children who have self-confidence and celebrate diversity. In fact, people who have self-confidence almost naturally celebrate diversity; they don't need to put down others to make themselves feel good. They feel proud of themselves every day. People who commit hate crimes or discriminate against others are often afflicted with low self-esteem. People who reach out to others, who work to make their communities better, their schools more nurturing, their culture more open, start with a confidence in themselves and project that feeling outward to everyone around them. We earn self-confidence by trying our best or using our self-control, and that colors everything we do in our lives. From Benjamin Franklin and Abraham Lincoln to Sojourner Truth and Mother Teresa, no one has ever made positive change in society without self-confidence. Without self-confidence, we are hurting our lives. We are hurting ourselves. In the musical *Bedknobs and Broomsticks*, the Sherman Brothers wrote:

*You must face the age of not believing,*
*doubting everything you ever knew,*
*until at last you start believing*
*there's something wonderful in you.*

We all have something truly wonderful in us, and it's up to us to acknowledge that, nurture it, and be proud of who we are.

# 8

# Responsibility and Consequences

A woman I know, a very distinguished leader in her community, has been embarrassed for years about what began as a relatively innocent deception. For years, she had headed her local garden club—growing plants was her hobby and her passion. She had also served as a trustee of a prestigious institution located in her town. One year, the institution's president unexpectedly resigned to take the top job at a major university. The trustees asked my friend to act as president until they could find a permanent replacement.

The garden club was depending on her to grow its entry in the local flower show. But she had no time to put in the careful work she normally would have, so in desperation she went to a local market and bought a good-looking geranium. To her dismay, it won the grand prize in the show.

To this day, she feels terrible about winning the prize; she realizes that what she did was wrong. She did not take responsibility for growing her own flower.

This reminds me of an experience from my own childhood. Effie tried to teach us about responsibility: We were in charge of cleaning our rooms and doing our homework. But, Effie loved us so much that she sometimes did things that we should have done ourselves. One year, when I was in grade school, our whole class was told to make Easter bonnets. I didn't make my own; Effie did it for me. It won first prize, and I've felt bad about it ever since. I didn't take responsibility for my actions.

Sometimes, it's hard for adults to let go and allow kids to take responsibility. When Andy started at a new school, I walked him to his classroom the first day. And the second day. While I was walking him there on the third day, he said, "Daddy, I'm fine on my own." And he was right. Although I meant well, I was being overprotective and needed to acknowledge the fact that Andy was capable of taking responsibility for himself.

Nowadays, it has become commonplace for many parents who mean well not just to help their children with homework but to do it for them. But are they really helping their kids by doing the work the children should be doing themselves? A friend's teenage son recently asked her, "Do we have waffles?" She answered that they did, the frozen kind.

"Can you make me some?" he asked.

"He had to walk by the freezer and the toaster to ask me the question," she recalls. "I told him he was old enough to make them himself."

Indulging kids by doing tasks that they are capable of doing themselves may be an easy way to keep them from complaining and avoiding conflict. But it infantilizes them and doesn't give them one of the best gifts adults can give children: responsibility. Kids whose parents do their math or spelling or geography may never learn how to multiply or do long division, how to spell "niece" or "pharmacy," or find out where Belgium is. At the same time, kids who demand things from their parents may never learn how to take care of themselves.

The definition of responsibility and consequences we give to kids is this:

*Responsibility is when I am able to take care of myself and depend on myself. A consequence is the result of what I do and what I say. I know I am responsible for whatever consequences result from my actions.*

Just like adults, children have responsibilities. When we go into classrooms, we ask the students to tell us what their responsibilities are. "I have to do my homework," said a boy in Wisconsin. Getting ready for school, doing their homework, and getting to school on time are answers we hear often. We explore the concept of responsibilities to help kids understand that they are, indeed, responsible for themselves. They shouldn't expect parents to do their homework, or siblings to walk their dog. And in today's society (understandably with our busy schedules), kids often have to take a larger role in household responsibilities. "I have to take care of my little sister," said a girl in a Washington classroom. How can we expect kids to do any of these things if we don't first teach them about responsibility?

When children understand responsibility, they also start to grasp the idea of consequences. Consequences are not punishments; they are simply the logical result of our actions or lack of action. With consequences we can make things happen or not happen. Put on sunscreen, and you won't burn. Don't put it on, and you'll get a sunburn and damage your skin. Take time for breakfast, and you'll feel energetic all morning. Don't eat breakfast, and you may be hungry and tired.

In a caring, supportive way, we teach the kids that they choose the consequences when they take responsibility, or when they don't. This way, children learn to take ownership of their responsibilities and the consequences that follow them.

Responsibility should be a part of our daily routine. One good way to teach that to children is to share with them adult experiences with using responsibility or not using it. I often tell kids about my experience with laundry. I sometimes get so caught up in my work that I leave my laundry to the last minute. Once, before leaving on a weeklong trip during which I was to teach the ABCs of Life at a school, I didn't take responsibility and waited until the last moment to do my laundry. The clothes were being dried on the morning of my flight. In a rush, I forgot to get my clothes out of the dryer. I left for the week without any pants except the ones I had on. I spent the week teaching in the same khaki jeans every day.

Another time I went out of town to a family event and once again waited until the last minute to pack. The consequence was that I ended up with two left shoes (one black sneaker and one black dress shoe). Not wanting to walk clockwise all day, I hunted around for someone with a similar shoe size who had an extra pair of shoes. Luckily, my brother-in-law had an extra pair of dress shoes, one size too small. The consequence was that I ended up with sore, blistered feet. I learned from my mistakes and now take responsibility to leave plenty of time to pack.

A teacher told her class the story of how she constantly puts her keys in different places. Since she did not take responsibility and have a regular place for her keys, the consequence was that she ultimately lost her keys. She had to get a locksmith to re-place them all.

The effect of this story on the children was striking. They loved hearing an adult admit to human foibles, to forgetting to take responsibility. Once they understand that adults make mistakes, you can introduce them to more serious concepts about failing to take responsibility: If you smoke, the consequence is that you could end up with lung, mouth, throat, or pancreatic cancer. If you take drugs, you could die. Taking responsibility can be a matter of life and death. My brother was in a serious car accident. Because he took the responsibility to wear a seat belt, he's alive today.

I can't emphasize enough how important it is for children and adults to share experiences. When adults talk about their responsibilities and the consequences that result, children see clearly that they are learning a skill that will remain with them throughout their lives. In the age-old story of Pinocchio, Pinocchio starts off by lying and disappearing with strangers. Then he learns to take responsibility and assume control of his life. In doing so, Pinocchio discovers and uses the skills he has and becomes human. If kids discover and use the skills they have, they will be able to lead healthy, safe, productive, and happy lives.

When first talking to kids about responsibility, begin with simple things they can relate to, like brushing their teeth, eating a good breakfast before school, watering the plants, or recycling. Ask them to think about what happens if they don't take on these responsibilities. They'll realize that not brushing their teeth can cause cavities; not watering the plants will make the plants wilt and die; not eating breakfast might make them hungry, cranky, and even sleepy during class. Explain that these are consequences—not punishments, just the normal, expectable results of certain actions. Kids may think they are getting away with staying up late, but the next day they will be too tired to do all the things they want to do. They are only hurting themselves.

We talk with children about consequences in their daily lives. If they do their homework, they learn more; if they don't do their homework, they learn less. We help them to see that they hurt themselves when they don't do their work. We ask kids, "Who gives you the grades on your report card?" Many kids say "the teacher" or "the principal." Then we remind them that the teacher only looks over their work. It's up to them to take responsibility for themselves and to study and to try their best. So who really gives them that grade? "We do," they reply.

It's up to children to remember that consequences are a result of what they do and what they say. They are not caused by their parents or their teachers. If they do a good job at home or at school, they are taking responsibility; they can be proud of themselves and feel self-confident. It's worth saying again: The skills are sequential. Self-confidence is a skill that can help build responsibility.

To help children internalize responsibility, it is important to provide consistency with your boundaries and structure. For example, if you and your child are taking a trip to the toy store, make your expectations and consequences clear before you enter the store. You can tell her that if she takes responsibility to use her self-control in the toy store, then the consequence may be that she can stay in the store longer. Then let her know if she doesn't take responsibility to use her self-control in the toy store (if she whines for a new toy or throws a tantrum), then the consequence is that she leaves the store immediately. To help children understand responsibility (and the limits you set), it's important to follow through with whatever consequences you have set up.

Parents have also shared that when your consequences relate to the responsibility at hand, children are more likely to take ownership of their actions. For example, if a child asks to ride his bicycle to a friend's house and takes responsibility to return back to your house by a certain time, then the consequence could be that he will have more freedom to ride his bicycle to other places. If he doesn't take responsibility to return home by a certain time, then the consequence could be that he will lose the privilege to ride his bike to his friend's house for a period of time.

It's important to make your expectations clear and match the consequences with the situation. By doing this, you are helping a child learn about accepting responsibility and its consequences.

Parents can talk with their kids about the responsibilities they have in everyday life. Explain to your kids that you have to go to work and do your job in order to make the money to provide the essentials of life. Or if you are a stay-at-home parent, explain that your responsibilities include looking after the well-being of the children, the running of the house, shopping, paying the bills, and so forth. Let them know that all adults have responsibilities to fulfill in order to keep their lives on an even keel.

One way to help children begin to comprehend the concept of responsibility is by helping them to understand the responsibility of others. We do this in a fun game called What's My Responsibility?

Think of a list of occupations with your child and write them on small pieces of paper (or Post-it notes). Choose one child to be the worker and stick the piece of paper on the child's forehead or back so that the worker cannot see the paper but everyone else can. Ask everyone else to take turns giving the worker clues about the profession. Adults and children should take turns being the worker.

Say things like, "It's your responsibility to take care of sick people." Remind children to use the word "responsibility." The game goes on until the worker guesses the job—in this case, doctor or nurse. Play this game to explore the concept of consequences and ask the child what the consequence might be if each worker did not take responsibility to do his or her job. What's important about this game—indeed, about all the games in the book—is that it relates to children on a level they can understand.

Once you have introduced the skill, either at home or at school, remind the kids of all of the things they need to take responsibility to do: from taking care of themselves to taking care of the environment. Reinforce the notion of responsibility until it becomes second nature. Also remind them that there are consequences to their actions. It's important to distinguish consequences from punishments; just let them know that the choice of consequence is up to them. What happens as a result of their actions is no one's decision or fault but their own. This is a lesson that will stay with them for life.

Another game we play with children is the Responsibility Challenge. Kids are on their own a lot and can practice taking responsibility for themselves through this challenging game. Whether adults are around or not, kids can learn to take responsibility on their own. Give a child a book to read (or she can pretend to be reading one) and tell her that her challenge is to take responsibility and use her self-control to stay focused on the book. Let her know that you might be walking around the room, talking to another adult, or even leaving the room, and she has to take responsibility for herself no matter what you are doing. The consequence for losing self-control—looking away from the book or talking to someone in the room—is a point for you. If she remains focused for five seconds, then the child (or group) receives a point. It is her responsibility to use her self-control whether an adult is watching her or not.

It's also important to remember while playing this game that no one is ever out, and it doesn't matter who wins or loses. What matters is that you try your best, taking responsibility. This game helps children understand that when they are on their own, it is up to them to take responsibility for their actions.

Years ago, one girl, unlike every other student in her class, forgot to bring her permission slip. As a result, instead of going on the class trip to the zoo, she spent the entire day sitting in the principal's office. "I told everyone who came in that I hadn't done anything wrong," she says. She understood that she wasn't being punished. The school administration was simply obeying regulations, and she was feeling the consequence of her failure to take responsibility. She regretted not taking that responsi-bility and missing out on that field trip. As an adult, one of the first things she did on her own was finally to visit the San Diego Zoo.

When I reached my senior year of high school, I met with the school guidance counselor. Since it was a preparatory school, I figured that the school's expertise in college placement would help point me toward the right college. To my dismay, all I got was a list of colleges that had nothing to do with my natural talents and abilities. I was discouraged yet energized to take matters into my own hands. I took the responsibility to buy a reference guide of all of the colleges in the country and stayed up all night reading it. I was excited when I finally came upon Emerson College.

I was enthralled by the discovery that it was a small school with a tradition of excellence in all the subjects I wanted to learn. It offered courses in public speaking, debate, drama, and education. When I got there, I was surrounded by enthusiastic teachers and fellow students. Henry (the Fonz) Winkler was a few years ahead of me; Jay Leno was in my class. After scraping by in secondary school, I suddenly found myself on the dean's list. By taking responsibility for my own life, I found a place in which I could finally excel. More important, I found a place where I could be myself.

As I was feeling good about one aspect of my life, I soon discovered that I needed to take responsibility for other areas of my life as well. Whenever I visited home, my parents were always too busy to pick me up at the airport. They were also too busy to spend time with me during my time at home. After Effie died, my visits to them began to feel like my childhood all over again, but this time without her love and comfort. I realized that I needed to take responsibility for my own happiness when I visited home, rather than feeling lonely and sorry for myself. So I decided to call my Aunt Fran and Uncle Leon. They would pick me up and let me stay at their apartment. With love, common sense, honesty, and humor, they would talk with me for hours about work and life. Uncle Leon even went to Coney Island with me. And, just as I did when I was a child, I made appointments to see my parents. Instead of wallowing in self-pity, though, I realized that I was the one who was responsible for making myself happy, not my parents. I couldn't expect them to be people they weren't.

Many teachers have told us anecdotes about kids who didn't take responsibility to speak up for themselves. Once, a teacher passed out workbooks to all of the kids in the class but forgot to give a workbook to one child. Instead of taking responsibility and speaking up, the child just sat there with nothing to do. At one point, the teacher looked around the room and noticed that this child was not working. She asked him why he wasn't working in his workbook and he replied that he didn't have one. She apologized and told the child that she had made a mistake. But she also noticed that he was too afraid to speak up for himself.

This happens often: Kids don't alert teachers to a problem or ask questions when they don't understand something because they're afraid of being judged. Their fear of what other people will think of them prevents them from taking responsibility for their actions. They're afraid to take care of themselves. This mentality permeates not only childhood; our world is filled with adults who have abandoned their dreams because they're too afraid of what other people will think of them. There are some adults who never asked questions in elementary school and still don't know the answers today.

Our society has created a culture of victimization, in which we blame others for the problems we find ourselves in. People sue fast-food chains, claiming that their food made them fat. An actress arrested for shoplifting explains that her director made her do it. A military officer accused of violating laws during the Iran-contra scandal says his superiors told him to. Spousal abusers routinely tell courts that the words of their spouses made them strike out. Schoolyard bullies say, "She made me hit her."

Taking responsibility shows awareness that we are in control of our actions and our lives. Even when we make mistakes, taking responsibility helps us to grow as well as to avoid the same mistakes in the future.

Blame, on the other hand, serves no purpose. It transfers control of our lives to others. It often results in self-pity and stagnation. Rather than assign blame, it is better to accept what has happened, learn from it, and move on.

Just recently, a seven-year-old girl took the responsibility to call the police on a cell phone while she and four other young children were trapped inside a car. Their drunken babysitter had passed out at a rest stop with the motor still running. The babysitter's blood alcohol level was almost three times the legal limit. These children took the responsibility to speak up for themselves and take care of themselves. They probably saved their own lives. But what about the very young who must depend on adults for most of their needs? How many stories must we hear about children left in car seats only to die from the oppressive heat? The consequences of not taking responsibility can be deadly.

As I travel around the country, I am saddened by the memorials I often see to teenagers who have lost their lives in drunken-driving accidents. If only they had internalized the skill of responsibility, they would have had the strength to avoid drinking, especially while they were behind the wheel of a car, or called someone to pick them up instead of riding in a car of a driver who had been drinking. While these youths were responsible enough to get their licenses, they weren't able to tap in to skills of self-control and feel enough self-confidence to make the responsible choices that may not have been popular with their friends. I recently read a story about a teenager who died because the driver of the car he was in was drunk. At the funeral, his mother read the story *Goodnight Moon* by Margaret Wise Brown, a favorite of the boy's from childhood. I couldn't help but think how devastating that was for the parents and how avoidable this nightmare was if only everyone had been responsible.

All people, young and old, need this skill. I once worked in an intergenerational program, which brought kids to a nursing home to visit and work and play with senior citizens. As one of our activities, we introduced the kids and the seniors to each other by the names we thought they liked to be called. We thought we knew what the seniors' names were, because they were written on cards outside their rooms.

We were shocked to find out that these were in fact not the names by which they liked to be called. Many of the names had been invented by the nursing home staff and randomly assigned to the residents without their consent. Fully one-third of the residents hated the names that were hanging on their door. After we talked with them about the issue, they became empowered enough to take responsibility to change things. Like the rejuvenated elders in the film *Cocoon*, they took responsibility, ripped up their nameplates, and had them replaced with the names they preferred. For many of them, taking responsibility was the first step in being treated with dignity and feeling self-respect. I've seen this happen in classrooms too, especially with children from different cultures. It's important for everyone to take responsibility for themselves and correct the mispronunciations of their names.

Responsibility is a vital skill in our society, as anyone who has dealt with the health system knows all too well. My son, Andy, was having trouble with his foot a few years ago, so Mimi and I took him to the hospital. The X-ray showed a space between bones on his foot; at the least, they said, he would need a cast. But Andy was only limping. He didn't think anything was broken, and neither did we. Not knowing what to do, we overheard an orthopedic surgeon being paged over the intercom. We im-

mediately took responsibility and asked that the orthopedic surgeon examine Andy's foot.

We asked him to reexamine the X-ray. He obliged us and
then started to chuckle. The space in the X-ray was normal for
a child, just an indication of the direction in which Andy's
foot would grow. He diagnosed a mild sprain, put an Ace band-
age on Andy, and sent him home. Had we not taken responsibility, Andy's minor injury would have been mistreated and
he might have gone around hobbled by a cast on his foot for
weeks.

Several years ago, I learned a very important lesson about
responsibility. I used to get nervous and overreact when cars
pulled up from side streets at intersections where I was driving.
Even though these cars were nowhere near my automobile, their
presence always made me flinch. Mimi noticed this and thought
it was important that I see an eye doctor. I finally did take responsibility, and the doctor told me that I had glaucoma, which
affects peripheral vision. Luckily, I had lost only 10 percent of
my vision. Had I not taken responsibility and gone at all, I could
have gone blind.

Adults are often the worst culprits at not taking responsibility for their health. From scheduling regular and specialized
exams and taking action when feeling sick to taking prescribed
medications, we often become very lax. Katie Couric, of the
*Today* show, is an inspiring example of a person being responsible for her own health. After her young husband, Jay Monahan,
lost his life to colon cancer, she began a nationwide campaign
that motivated thousands of people to take responsibility and
get a colonoscopy. Procedures like this one can save lives.

The easiest thing in the world is to avoid responsibility. You
can tell your boss that you didn't finish a job because the materi-

als didn't arrive, or that you didn't do a report because you didn't get the information on time. Of course, you could have called the suppliers and asked where the bricks and mortar were, or called the accounting department to ask for the figures, but it was easier to just sit back and pin the blame on someone else. This tendency to duck responsibility permeates our culture: Kids still tell their teachers that the dog ate their homework to get out of doing what they're supposed to.

In the past few decades, a new kind of criminal trial has become almost commonplace. Two juries hear one trial of two defendants, each of whom claims that the other is responsible for the crime. Saying that somebody else made you do anything—from fighting in the schoolyard to fraud to cheating to murder—is an abdication of responsibility, a sign that our culture hasn't taught this skill to its young people and encouraged it throughout their lives. We can stop this cycle by defining, teaching, and modeling responsibility to young children. We could have a society of adults and children who admit mistakes when they make them, even when they've tried their best. We could have politicians who don't engage in cover-ups but stand up and tell the truth. We could have merchants and executives who don't hide behind a phalanx of lawyers and a smokescreen of public relations but simply admit, "I was wrong." Taking responsibility is a form of courage that can transform an excuse-driven society.

## Teaching the ABCs of Life:
## Responsibility and Consequences

### 1: *INTRODUCE AND DEFINE IT*

**Responsibility is when I am able to take care of myself and depend on myself. A consequence is the result of what I do and what I say. I know I am responsible for whatever consequences result from my actions.**

After cutting out the responsibility and consequences poster in the appendix, read the definition aloud together and introduce responsibility and consequences. Here are some suggestions.

"Responsibility means taking care of ourselves. When we take responsibility, we can either make things happen or not happen—we call those things consequences. If you have gym class, you take responsibility to remember the right clothes. If you don't take responsibility, the consequence is that you are not able to participate. If you do take responsibility, the consequence is that you may play in gym class. I have the responsibility to feed the fish. If I don't take responsibility to do that, then the consequence is that the fish could die. If I do take responsibility to feed the fish, then the consequence is that the fish will be healthy. Responsibility can have serious consequences. If we don't take responsibility to wear a seat belt, the consequence is that we can be seriously hurt.

"When you take responsibility, the consequence is that you have more freedom to take more responsibility in the future. It's exciting to take responsibility because it gives you a feeling of independence, showing you can handle more situations on your own."

## 2: EXPERIENCE IT
### What's My Responsibility?

What does it mean to be responsible? This question can be hard for kids to answer. This game is an easy way to start to understand the concept of responsibility, because children identify the responsibilities of others. And once they do that, it is easier for them to understand their own responsibilities and what the word "responsibility" means.

1. Work together to create a list of occupations with which the children are familiar. This list can include professions like firefighter, nurse, doctor, teacher, police officer, lifeguard, or basketball player.
2. Write the name of each occupation—or draw a picture if children are too young to read—on a small piece of paper (Post-it notes work well).
3. Choose one child to be the worker. Stick the piece of

paper on the child's forehead or back so that the worker cannot see the paper but the rest of the game's players can. You can play too!

4.  Have the other players who can see the paper take turns giving the worker clues about the profession. Players can say things like, "It's your responsibility to take care of sick people," or "It's your responsibility to watch people at the beach." Remind players to use the word "responsibility" and to have fun and try their best when they give clues.

5.  While children give clues, have the worker guess the occupation. Remind workers to have fun and to keep trying, even if they can't think of the occupation right away. It's okay if they make a mistake, as long as they try their best.

6.  Switch roles so that everyone, including you, gets a chance to be the worker.

FURTHER SUGGESTION

•  A version of this game for older children is to give the worker a slightly different role. Instead of the other players telling the worker what she does, the worker asks the rest of the players questions about what she does. The rest of the players take turns answering the questions with yes or no. The worker can ask questions like, "Is it my responsibility to help children?" "Is it my responsibility to rescue people?" "Is it my responsibility to keep the city clean?" "Is it my responsibility to memorize lines?" The game goes on until the worker guesses the occupation. Remind children to use the word "responsibility" and to have fun and try their best when they ask questions and when they answer questions too.

After playing the game, discuss the following:

- What are some responsibilities you have in your life?

Remind children to follow the Pledge for Success when they talk about responsibility in this game. They should celebrate diversity no matter what occupation they are talking about, and they should use their listening skills when other children are talking about responsibility.

## Responsibility Challenge

Sometimes, as soon as the teacher's back is turned, or the boss leaves your office, it's awfully easy to stop taking responsibility. But we all need to learn how to take responsibility for ourselves even when it's tempting not to do so. This game allows children to practice taking responsibility for themselves even when there are distractions.

1. Let the children know that you are going to challenge them to take responsibility and use their self-control.
2. Have them pretend to read a book (or they can get a real book). Explain that you might be walking around the room, talking to another adult, or even leaving the room (you can peek in the doorway). Explain that it is their responsibility to use their self-control to focus on the book. This is the same responsibility it takes to do their schoolwork and homework.
3. Explain that the consequence for looking away or talking to someone in the room is a point for you. If they take responsibility and remain focused for five seconds, then the children get a point.
4. Start the game by saying, "Responsibility challenge, begin."

5. Walk around the room, talk to someone else, or leave the room for a few moments. Remember that no one is ever out. Everyone is trying his or her best to take responsibility.

6. End the game by saying, "Responsibility challenge over."

FURTHER SUGGESTIONS:

- Once children are taking responsibility for themselves while you are not watching them, you can make the game more challenging. You can make sounds, talk to the children, or make any other distractions. In this version of the game, you are challenging everyone to take responsibility to not look up, laugh, or respond to your antics.

After playing the game, discuss the following:

- Whose responsibility is it to make sure you use your self-control? Who made you look up and lose your self-control?
- What are some distractions you have when you're trying to do your homework?
- What are some ways you can take responsibility when you're on your own?
- What is something you can do if you're not focused that can help you calm down, so that you can take responsibility to do your homework? (Self-Control Time)

## 3: SHARE IT
### Share Stories About Responsibility

As you begin to think about sharing from your own life, here are some anecdotes that friends, colleagues, and people from around the country have shared with me. Please share these stories and your own stories about responsibility and consequences, and ask kids to share their stories about responsibility and consequences too.

A teacher had told me that after his students had repeatedly neglected to turn their homework in on time, he gave them the assignment to write an essay on responsibility, and he gave the class three days to do it. Each day, he reminded them to take responsibility to work on their essays so that they would be finished in time. Each day, he used the word "responsibility" in the directions he gave: take responsibility to return from recess on time, take responsibility to leave the computer lab just as orderly as they had found it. And when the children handed in their essays on Friday afternoon, the teacher put them in his briefcase and headed home on the train. It took him until Saturday morning to realize that he had left his briefcase, and the students' essays, on the train. On Monday, he told the class that he hadn't taken responsibility to take care of his briefcase and their essays, and he was going to write an essay on responsibility too. (He called the Lost and Found Office later that day and it turned out they had the briefcase.)

At a family workshop, one man said that a few weeks before, he had spent a Saturday afternoon swimming at the beach with his friends. When they returned to his car, he realized that his keys had been in the pocket of his bathing suit all day. Since the door opener was electronically powered, the keys were ruined by the water, so no one could get into the car. One friend had a baby who needed changing, and the rest of the diapers were in the car too. When they tried to break into the car, the alarm went off, which scared the wet and tired infant to tears. Eventually, the police came and helped him get into the car. The man admitted that the end of the day would have been a lot more relaxing if he had taken responsibility to keep his keys in a safe place.

A girl told me that she recently had plans to play with a friend after school, but at the last minute, the friend canceled. So the girl went home instead. She looked for the key her parents hid underneath the birdhouse on their porch, but it wasn't there. So she went down the street to a different friend's house and called her own house and left a message on the voice mail, which her parents were supposed to check, telling them that she was locked out and would wait at her friend's house until they came to get her. But it took a long time for them to come, and when they did, they said that they had been so worried about where she was that they had forgotten to check the voice mail. So from now on, she said, they are both going to take responsibility: She is going to continue telling her parents where she is on the voice mail, and they are going to leave the key where it's supposed to be and check the voice mail more often.

Andy kept asking my wife and me to let him have a dog. We kept telling him how much responsibility it was to have a pet. He said he'd be able to take care of the dog. So we went to the pet store and decided on a little white Maltese, whom we named Spunky. But one night, Andy hadn't felt like walking the dog. And when Andy woke up that morning, he had to clean up the mess that Spunky had made. Once Andy realized the consequences of not walking the dog, he took responsibility to take better care of Spunky.

## Responsibility Discussion Starters

Both adults and kids have responsibilities. Some of our responsibilities include eating healthy snacks, cleaning our rooms, using self-control, and studying for a spelling test. These are jumping-off points for casual conversations with your kids about the skill of responsibility. Here are some good ideas to reinforce the topic.

- Discuss your responsibilities. Begin by saying, "I take responsibility to . . ." Discuss the consequences of taking responsiblity or not taking responsibility.
- Discuss responsibilites that every member of the family has. Explore how these responsibilities help the family run smoothly.
- Who controls what grades you receive on your report card? Discuss how the teacher just looks over your work. You earn the grades yourself by either taking or not taking responsibility to try your best.
- Older kids may confuse the word "consequence" with "punishment." Get a discussion going on the idea by asking, "What is the first thing you think of when you hear the word 'consequences'?" Younger children may not know the meaning of the word "consequence." Explain that consequences are not punishments, they are the result of what we do or what we don't do.
- Talk about the fact that we all choose our consequences by deciding either to take responsibility or not take responsibility. To give an example kids will understand, you can tell them that it is their responsibility to clean their room. If they take responsibility to clean their room, then the consequence is that they can invite a few of their friends for a sleepover, because their room is clean enough for guests to sleep in. If they don't take responsibility to clean their room, then the consequence is that they won't be able to have their friends for a sleepover, because, in a messy room, their friends will have no place to sleep.

- What is the consequence if you eat breakfast and the consequence if you don't eat breakfast? (You either have energy for your day or not.) Questions like this help kids think about the meaning and consequences of their actions. Continue asking children what the consequences are for many of their daily responsibilities (homework, waking up on time, cleaning up, etc.).
- Discuss the responsibilities you both have at home, school, or work.
- Ask children to describe what's wrong with this statement: "My mother forgot to put my homework in my bag."
- Have a discussion about responsibilities relating to safety. For example, you can discuss the importance of calling 911 during emergencies.
- What is one responsibility you have a hard time keeping? What can you do to make sure you take responsibility for it in the future?

### Skill Builders for Adults and Children

- Think of someone you recently saw or heard about who took responsibility.
- Think of someone you recently saw or heard about who did not take responsibility. What could the person have done differently?
- Think of a time in the last week when you took responsibility.
- When did you not take responsibility but wish you had? What could you have done differently?
- Have a conversation about role models—people you know who take responsibility.

- The skills are everywhere. Give an example of a book, movie, current event, or television show where people or characters either took or didn't take responsibility.

## Helpful Hints

Have children reflect on the school subjects they are naturally good at and others with which they need more practice. Remind them that they need to take responsibility to work harder at the subjects they find more difficult. You can let children know the areas where you naturally excel, as well as the areas that you need to take more responsibility for.

Think of different scenarios throughout the day when children can take responsibility. Although children use responsibility every day, designate a "Responsibility Day," so children get to practice and understand what responsibility is. For example, you can ask your child to take responsibility to go to the store and buy some things that the family needs. If she does take responsibility and uses the money that you give her to buy the items that the family needs, and brings home a receipt and the correct change, then the consequence is that she will be able to do something like this again. If she does not take responsibility and buys herself extra things with the money that you have given her, then the consequence is that she will not be able to take other excursions like this in the immediate future.

Responsibility activities are great for home and school alike. Teachers can play the Responsibility Challenge on a day before they know they will be absent and a substitute teacher will be in their place. Parents can play the game before a babysitter comes over. It's a strong reminder to help children realize that whether you're there or not, they should take responsibility for themselves by using their self-control.

In some situations, you can help children take ownership of their actions by asking them to help you decide on a suitable consequence for either taking or not taking reponsibility. However, it's important to monitor the appropriateness of the consequences upon which they decide.

An American secretary of state and a British foreign minister resigned because of failed policies. A talk show host said that he was responsible for the failure of his program. The president of a major university quit because of actions others had taken during his tenure as a laboratory director. Any one of them could have weaseled out of the situation, pleaded his own innocence, blamed others, and hung on to an important job. But they didn't; they took responsibility. (By the way, they all went on to distinguished careers, opportunities given to them by people who respected them for taking responsibility.)

Consequences can be positive, but they can also sometimes be unpleasant. Even so, not taking responsibility is worse. Because these people accepted the consequences of their actions, they moved on to new success. But remember, the consequences of our actions can be rewarding as well. Study for the test, you do well. Rehearse for the concert, you perform at your best. Practice for the game, you make a strong showing. By choosing whether to take responsibility or not, you can make things happen or not happen.

It's up to us to take responsibility and own up to the consequences of our actions. We have to reinstill in our culture the notion that responsibility is a sign of strength, not weakness.

# 9

# Thinking and Problem Solving

We use thinking and problem solving every day. Children and adults constantly confront challenges at home, at school, in the community, at work, and everywhere in between. Rather than seeing a dead end when faced with a problem, we can use this skill to imagine all the fascinating choices and endless possibilities that are available to us. Thinking and problem solving together help us cure diseases, solve crimes, build structures, and write plays. Einstein used this skill to explain some of the basic structure of the universe; Bach and Mozart used it to compose melodies so complex they seem natural.

Frank Lloyd Wright is generally recognized as the greatest architect in America, at least since Thomas Jefferson. Yet even he faced difficult challenges that required thinking and problem solving. He was commissioned to build a house by a stream in western Pennsylvania. The easy thing to do would be to build on one side of the stream or the other, but he wanted to take advantage of the spectacular vistas the site afforded. After much thought, and hard design work, he came up with an unprecedented solution: He built the house over the stream. The water actually runs under it. He had solved a problem in a way that created an architectural masterpiece called Fallingwater, which, even though it is located in the rural and hard-to-find little village of Ohiopyle, is visited by tens of thousands of people every year.

This is what makes this skill so attractive and empowering: Once you internalize it, you can use every last ounce of your talent to best effect, whether in great enterprises or everyday events. You can use it to decide what to cook for dinner; the Egyptians used it to design the pyramids. Where you planted your backyard garden and how NASA got humans to the moon are both results of this skill. If you're playing chess or doing a crossword puzzle, building a kitchen or baking a soufflé, performing surgery or writing a legal brief, you're utilizing this skill.

We use it to solve personal dilemmas as well as to make everyday decisions. Say you have three errands to run in different parts of town. The first thing you do is think about the route that will allow you to drive the least possible distance in the shortest possible time; then you plot out the route and the time it will take. That's thinking and problem solving. If you plan a menu for your family's dinner, you think about how to balance food groups and decide which dishes work well together. When you choose a pair of shoes that will go well with a dress, or a tie that will go well with a suit, you're using your thinking and problem-solving skills.

Often, we have a tendency to feel stuck when confronted with a problem. That's where this skill comes in. If we are less intimidated by the ideas of thinking and problem solving and start to look at our problems as provocative challenges, we can begin to solve them. When confronted with problems, we need to focus on the process of thinking. We should be inspired by the fact that we have the capacity to work through the problem, try out solutions, and try new solutions if others don't work out the way we want them to.

The best way to help kids first understand thinking and problem solving is by defining it.

*Thinking is when I come up with as many ideas as I can. Problem solving is when I think in order to solve a problem. I keep thinking until I solve the problem. I never give up.*

All too often, adults—whether parents, teachers, or caretakers—categorize and label kids. They might say, for example, that there are some children who are smart and some who are not smart. Very early on, Lesson One dispels that notion. We talk to children about how every child is smart as long as he or she takes responsibility to use his or her brain to think. Without confidence in their own intelligence, some children might believe that thinking and problem solving is a skill that is simply beyond their grasp. It's not, and it's important for us to communicate that fact.

With some of my teachers at school telling me I was stupid and that I did only average work, I was pretty convinced that I was bad at math too. I didn't pick up on concepts as quickly as some of the other kids, and I was well on my way to believing that I never would. Then I met Mr. Dupee.

At first, I was bored and frustrated in Mr. Dupee's class. I took to making spitballs and shooting them from the rubber bands on my braces. Like any good teacher, Mr. Dupee had eyes in the back of his head, and he caught me.

This was the perfect opportunity to embarrass me in front of my peers, to make an example of me and humiliate me before the class. To my amazement, he didn't take it. Instead, he launched into a discussion of the spitball's trajectory; he helped me to calculate its arc and its rate of speed. Suddenly, I saw that math was not just some bland, boring, abstract subject, but a way to look at the physical world. He helped me to understand that thinking and problem solving was fun.

I trusted Mr. Dupee to treat me with respect, so I wasn't afraid to ask him what some teachers might have mocked as a stupid question. I asked his help in understanding a math concept. Although I could understand complex math concepts, sometimes I had a hard time understanding the simplest commonsense ideas. One of the toughest concepts I had to deal with in math was multiplying by zero. If you multiply 8 by zero, for example, the answer is zero, but I wondered: Where did the 8 go? Mr. Dupee explained that 8 x 0 simply meant that there were eight zeros. Once I thought about that, I understood it. Once I understood it, I could start solving problems. I became a much better math student. It's important not just to know the answer but also to understand the reason behind the concept.

For some adults, thinking and problem solving becomes a way of life—and a source of satisfaction. Jill Fredston and Doug Fesler, a husband-and-wife team who codirect the Alaska Mountain Safety Center, spend their summers rowing through the Arctic Circle. "What we like about it is that it's not figured out," he says. "It's a land you have to figure out on your own." Using their thinking and problem-solving skills, they have covered twenty-two thousand miles of the most desolate and beautiful coastline on Earth.

As we explain to kids, thinking and problem solving is not just an intellectual skill; it comes into play in daily life, in relations with others. But most important, it's about process and about choices. We don't want anybody ever to feel stuck, whether it's about what college to attend, what career to choose, or even what hairstyle to get or book to read. The process allows us to choose, try again, and continue challenging ourselves until we are happy with the outcome. From the time we get up in the morning until the time we go to bed at night, we need to know that we have the capability to defeat a problem rather than having the problem defeat us. When we use thinking and problem solving, fireworks seem to go off in our brains when we feel the powerful energy of finding the many ways we have to solve problems.

In the Harry Potter books by J. K. Rowling, the Hogwarts children use magic to solve the many problems that arise in their lives. Children need to know that although they don't have magic, they do have skills. Using their brains to think and solve problems is all the magic they need.

Thinking and problem solving, along with the other skills, can help improve academic performance as well. A third-grader was taking a test required of all students at her grade level. "I used the ABCs of Life when we were taking the test, as I tried to figure out the answer," she recalls. "I thought of all the possibilities and picked one. I tried my best." Studying the question, thinking about it, and trying to solve the problem—along with trying her best—helped her do well on the test.

How did the kids in the film *E.T.* protect their newfound friend from outer space? They thought about how best to conceal him and nestled him in among a pile of stuffed animals. Then, when the authorities were on his trail, they formed a bicycle convoy to smuggle him past the police and back to his home.

Granted, these scenes were brought to the screen by Steven

Spielberg, an adult—albeit one who has never lost his childlike wonder—but they accurately portray the kind of ingenuity kids can develop when they apply thinking to solving problems. Use examples like these when you talk to your kids about thinking and problem solving; it'll help make the idea more tangible.

In everyday life, we naturally use our thinking and problem-solving skills in activities like deciding what to wear, playing games such as chess or checkers, finding movies to rent or books to read. Instead of sitting around on a Saturday feeling bored, think of the wide variety of activities you could engage in. It's exciting to think of all the possibilities and choices we have.

> *Disaster didn't stymie Louis Pasteur!*
> *Edison took years to see the light!*
> *Alexander Graham knew failure well; he took a lot of knocks to*
> *    ring that bell!*
> *So when it gets distressing it's a blessing!*
> *Onward and upward you must press!*
> *Till up from the ashes, up from the ashes, grow the roses of*
> *    success.*

This Sherman Brothers song reminds me that we all make mistakes, we all feel frustrated, and it's okay to feel that way. In my mind this is what thinking and problem solving is all about. The important thing is to continue to use your thinking and never give up.

When introducing thinking and problem solving, we need to teach children that it's just as important to keep their brains in shape as it is to keep their bodies in shape. It's natural for us to stretch our bodies before running, but what about warming up our brains to think and solve problems? It doesn't make sense that this isn't done regularly before doing homework, working on a school subject, and brainstorming ways to solve a personal problem. The following activities are great warm-ups that give children the opportunity to "exercise" their brain before they get started with the challenge at hand. You can start by asking kids how many items they can name in a particular category. For example, ask for things that are green.

Right away, you'll hear grass and leaves, but keep gently challenging them to think of more ideas. Perhaps one child will come up with dinosaurs. Another might say lizards. Another might remember an Easter egg or a St. Patrick's Day flag, the kitchen counter at home or her mom's car or—if you happen to live in San Francisco—even the sports section of the daily newspaper. No matter how improbable or particular these answers are, they all are good. If you keep children excited and involved, you'll get a variety of answers, ranging from the Incredible Hulk to the moon.

Use what they're studying in school to help them develop this skill. Say they're reading about Egypt; ask them things they might find there. Encourage them, and they'll tick off mummies, and pyramids, and deserts, and the Sphinx. Challenge them for more, and you might get the Nile, and camels, and maybe even hieroglyphics. The point is that when you unleash children's ability to think, they come up with remarkable ideas and solutions. Their minds and imaginations start to work, fueled by unstoppable energy.

Another simple warm-up takes just a piece of paper or a

chalkboard. All you need to do is draw a little pictogram. It could look something like this:

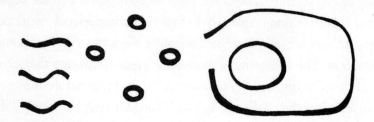

Then just let their thinking and imagination run loose. Some of them may see a face; others may see planets revolving around the sun. Balls being juggled, parts of a baseball diamond. Once they start thinking, they may see possibilities that never occurred to them before.

In my masters' program, I worked extensively with Fritz Bell, a mentor and pioneer of teaching through play and experience. At one workshop, he gave everybody strands of yarn and asked us to make pictures. He encouraged us to be creative and to use our imagination. We had a great time—and became playful and energized and, yes, even childlike—as we manipulated the strands into works of art. And we were adults.

This also showed me that you can use everyday materials to teach the skills. You can play Create a Picture with yarn, Pick-Up Sticks, pipe cleaners, etc. It helps kids to recapitulate many of the things they have already learned in Lesson One: They use their self-control when they wait until everybody playing has materials. They use their self-confidence when they create designs that are unique to them. But most of all, they use their thinking and problem solving when they create designs. You can ask children to make a flower. Many kids will do a simple, daisylike design, with two vertical sticks and a starburst pattern of sticks arrayed around the top. Some will do tulips, bursting out in a V pattern from the top of a vertical stem. Often you will be amazed by the creativity and distinctiveness of the kids' creation. As they look at the work of others, remind them to respect the diversity of their designs. All the ideas, whether simple or complex, represent the work of people who are trying their best and using their self-confidence and self-control to accomplish something.

When playing these games, you never know what kids will come up with. Often their answers and ideas lead to teachable moments. One first-grader, during Create a Picture, made a design that I couldn't decipher. She told me that she had made a martini glass. I wondered what the stick on top of the picture was, and she told me it was the stick for the olive. Enter the teachable moment. A discussion immediately followed about drinks that are appropriate for adults and kids and how we all have to use our self-control. As you play the games and share the skills, you can easily wrap one skill around the other and refer back to previous skills. Even though we were talking about thinking, a discussion about self-control became a natural extension.

It's important to reiterate that the skills are sequential. By the time we reach thinking and problem solving, kids are continuing to integrate everything they have learned since their first experience with the Pledge for Success into a coherent whole. Their ABCs of Life are now crystallizing as a unified way of dealing with themselves and with others.

Not everybody is predisposed to thinking. Many adults go through life with rote responses to situations, and the older they get, the less they seem to use their minds. I noticed that phenomenon once in a nursing home I worked in. Many of the older men were unengaged, lacking intellectual stimulation. We hit on the idea of showing them old movies and asking them about the period in which the films were made and finding out what they knew about the cast members. That helped, but we still had trouble getting them to read. Some of them said they didn't want to read but would gladly look at magazines with pictures of women—something the home's administration wanted no part of.

One Sunday, I used my own thinking and problem-solving skills while reading the *New York Times Magazine.* I noticed that many of the ads were for fashion items, from fur coats to lingerie. It occurred to me that the older men in the nursing home might look at the pictures and then be drawn into the articles.

It worked. The pictures of attractive women were the draw that brought them into the magazine, but the men stayed with it. Soon, almost all of them were requesting copies, and they were reading it cover to cover. The staff, which had been skeptical that a group of people trained in elementary education would have anything to offer to a home filled with seniors, was amazed by the enthusiasm with which the men took to reading the articles from the *New York Times Magazine,* thinking about them, and discussing them among themselves. Our success with this simple exercise led the nursing home administration to renew our contract.

When I took a dance-therapy class, I learned that there are many ways to move the various parts of the body. When the teacher asked us to move our heads, most of us rigidly moved just up, down, and side to side. I learned after further movement classes that you can move your head in many different ways: rotate it, shake it, tilt it, stretch it, bob it up and down. This has been invaluable in teaching kids to play some of the ABCs of

Life games, but it has also helped me to understand, and teach, that there are many ways of thinking about almost any situation you confront in life.

One of the students in the class, Roberta, held a party at her house. We were young, struggling, and burdened by tuition bills, like a grad student version of the characters in *La Bohème* or *Rent*. When I got to Roberta's apartment, I saw that she had only some carpeting and a bunch of pillows scattered around the floor. In no time, all of us adjusted to this innovative way of decorating. We discovered that it is actually a lot of fun to lie around on pillows, to get a new perspective on how people can live and design their homes. If you use your thinking and problem solving, you don't need to be stuck in old patterns. Roberta reminded me that just as we can learn to move our bodies in new and inventive ways, we can think in new and inventive ways. To this day, I have throw pillows in an unfurnished area of my house, and I love it.

Each of us has a center, an internal focus that gives us a unique view of the world. We can use our uniqueness to think of all the possibilities that exist to solve the problems that confront us and create choices that are right for us, instead of doing what others think we should do. When confronted by problems—personal or work- or school-related—we must always keep in mind that we have the ability to take the world by storm. If we use thinking and problem solving as an integral part of our way of life, we can overcome any obstacle that stands in our way. We can look forward to the everyday challenges because we can experience the process of thinking and problem solving. It's thinking that helps us solve these problems to make a difference in our own lives and the lives of others.

## Teaching the ABCs of Life:
## Thinking and Problem Solving

· · · · · · · · · · · · · · · · · · · · · · · · · · · · · · · · · · · · · · · · · · · · ·

### 1: *INTRODUCE AND DEFINE IT*

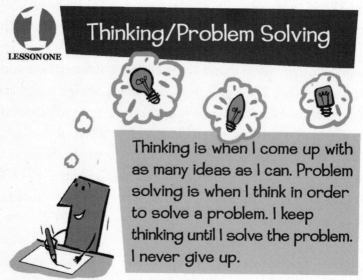

**Thinking/Problem Solving**

LESSON ONE

Thinking is when I come up with as many ideas as I can. Problem solving is when I think in order to solve a problem. I keep thinking until I solve the problem. I never give up.

After cutting out the thinking and problem solving poster in the Appendix, read the definition aloud together and introduce thinking and problem solving. Here are some suggestions.

"When we use our thinking, we come up with all the ideas that we can so that we can solve a problem. We're all smart, when we take responsibility to use our brains to think. When we think, you and I will come up with as many ideas as we can and then pick one—it's like fireworks going off in our brains. So instead of saying that I can't think of anything to cook for dinner tonight, I use my thinking to come up with all the possibilities and then pick one. And it's the same for you. If your teacher tells you to write a story, instead of saying that you don't know what to write, think of all of the possibilities and then pick one. When we think and problem-solve, it's exciting, because instead of feeling stuck we can use our creativity to think of the endless possibilities, which makes things fun and challenging."

## 2: EXPERIENCE IT
### Brain Push-Ups

Have you ever found an answer in the last place you thought it would be? Thinking in new and innovative ways—the catch-phrase these days is "thinking outside of the box"—means using creativity to help us solve problems. This game will help show children how.

1. Start by introducing the game. Tell the children that you're going to challenge their thinking skills. Then give the children a specific category and challenge them to think of all of the possible things that could fit into that category. For example, you might challenge them to think of things that are circles, or that begins with the letter "b."

2. Ask the children to think of every item they can within that category. Gently remind them not to give up after the first one or two items they think of. Tell them how important it is not to feel stuck when you have a problem to solve; the idea is to think of all the ways you can solve the problem.

3. When the children have had success with some of the concrete categories you have named, continue the game with more challenging categories. Examples include bodies of water, zoo animals, state capitals, and games.

4. Encourage kids to use their thinking to come up with all the possibilities they can.

5. Don't forget that the children can also challenge you and your thinking. It's important for them to understand that thinking and problem solving is a skill adults use too. So let them challenge you with categories, and try your best to use your thinking.

After playing the game, discuss the following:

• What are some times when you might have to think creatively? (while doing homework, when having a problem with a brother or sister, doing an art project, etc.)

Reiterate the fact that this skill is an important way to make progress in difficult situations. Instead of feeling stuck when you have a problem, you can think and devise a number of ways to solve it.

## What Else Can This Be?

There are many ways to solve one problem. When we look at thorny situations—whether homework assignments, quarrels with friends, or difficulties at home—from a variety of perspectives, we often find solutions we would have never initially thought of. This game teaches children to think of all of the varied possibilities or answers that a problem could have.

1. Before you begin, you need some sort of stick: a ruler, a paper towel roll, a walking stick, or even a broomstick. Start by holding up the stick so that children can see it and explain to them that their challenge is to think of all of the things the stick could be.

2. To get the children started, tell them what you think it

could be. For example, it could be a flagpole, or a baseball bat, or the trunk of an elephant.

3. Ask the children to use their thinking and problem solving to come up with many ideas for what the stick could be. You can contribute other ideas too.

FURTHER SUGGESTIONS

- You might use sounds to challenge children's thinking. You can crumple a piece of paper, or, if you have a rain stick, turn it over so that it makes a noise. Ask the children to think of all of the things that the sound they are hearing might be, like rain, applause, static, etc. Remind them to have fun and be creative. (You can make a rain stick by putting unpopped popcorn, dried beans, rice, or beads inside a paper towel roll, then sealing off both ends of the tube. The sound it makes when you shake it is a crucial part of the game. Rain sticks are also available in toy stores.)

- To further challenge children's thinking, place one object in a bag. Have the kids place their hand inside the bag to guess what the object is. Try it with two objects, then three. Keep adding objects to challenge kids' thinking. Then challenge children to make bags of their own so that you can guess too.

- You can also vary the game by holding up other objects, like a ball, a sheet of paper, a beanbag, etc. Children can hold up some items that they've found, too.

- You can play another version of this game by doing the following: With your child, draw a picture or cut one out from a magazine. Then cover up most of the picture with another piece of paper, while leaving a portion visible. With your child, use thinking and problem solving to think of all the other things that the picture could be.

After playing the game, discuss the following questions:

- What should you do if you have a problem? Discuss how we use our thinking to think of all the possibilities and then pick one.
- When do you have to solve problems at home, at school, and in the neighborhood? Is it possible to solve a problem in different ways?

It may seem that these questions have little to do with shaking sticks and crumpling paper, but in fact they do. Make the connection for the kids between using their thinking and problem-solving skill to play the game and using it to solve real-life problems.

## Create a Picture

As we all know, life is full of problems. At a young age we begin to learn how we can solve our own problems through our thinking skills. Here is a game that helps children think of the varieties of ways in which we can solve problems. When we can think of a variety of solutions, we are not only able to solve the problems, but we also feel confident in our ability to handle any problems in life.

1. Before you begin the game, gather enough Pick-Up Sticks, popsicle sticks, pipe cleaners, or pieces of yarn so that each player can have eight to ten of the item. This game is for kids and adults, so be sure that you have enough for everyone, including yourself.
2. Give each player eight to ten pieces of whatever material you choose. Tell the children that their challenge is to use their thinking and problem solving to create something out of their materials.

3. Give players a simple, concrete object to make from the materials. You can ask children to make objects like a kite, a house, or a television. Allow two minutes for everyone to design his or her object. Remind them that a big part of this exercise is having fun using their thinking.

4. While the players are working, remind them that everyone is using his or her thinking to solve the problem and that different people solve problems in different ways. It's important to let kids know that there is no wrong way or right way to make the object. They just need to try their best.

5. Remind everyone not to feel stuck and give up. Instead, keep thinking to solve the problem.

6. Be creative. When the children have had success creating concrete objects, choose more complex objects, like flowers, their initials, a face, an animal, etc.

7. Next, have the players create a picture of their choice out of the materials. Have them use their thinking to think of all the possibilities of objects or designs and to pick one. Remind them that one thing is not better than another— we celebrate diversity.

8. Give the children a chance to come up with an object for everyone to design.

FURTHER SUGGESTION

- If playing in a classroom or with a large group, start by telling the children that one challenge is to use their self-control and not touch the materials until the directions are given. Explain that if they are not using their self-control, the consequence is that the material will be taken away. When the children get their self-control back, they will get the materials back. Reinforce the idea to the children that whether or not they play this game is up to them. When a child who lost his self-control gets it back, remind him that it's up to him to use self-control and that he should be proud of himself for getting it back. It is up to the child if he gets to play the game. When a child has regained his self-control, he can play the game again.

After playing the game, discuss the following questions:

- If you feel stuck while solving a problem, what should you do?
- Where else do you have to use your thinking to solve problems?

Take some time to discuss these questions with the kids. It's important that they understand, as they go along in their learning of the skills, that what they are learning is sequential. Respect for others and for diversity is not something they learn one day and forget the next; it is a crucial building block for thinking and problem solving. Self-confidence and self-control are also important elements of this skill. Get them thinking about how everything they have learned up till now supports the skill we are discussing.

## 3: SHARE IT
### Share Stories About Thinking and Problem Solving

As you begin to think about sharing from your own life, here are some anecdotes that friends, colleagues, and people from around the country have shared with me. Please share these stories and your own stories about thinking and problem solving, and ask kids to share their stories about thinking and problem solving too.

A teacher at a school I visited was going on maternity leave. Before she left school to go have her baby, her coworkers told her that they wanted to take her out to lunch. But the woman couldn't decide on where to go. First, they called a Japanese restaurant, but it was closed for lunch. Then they tried a French restaurant, but it was fully booked. Then they saw a review of a Mediterranean restaurant in the local paper, but when they called it, a recording said that the restaurant would not be opened until 4 P.M. The woman almost called off the lunch, but she knew that she had many hungry coworkers who really wanted to go out. So she decided on pizza, and the second Italian restaurant they called was open. The food was delicious, she said, and they even gave her a cupcake for dessert. The woman was glad that she hadn't given up, because she and her coworkers would have missed a lovely lunch.

When one of my friends bought her first new car, she made a hasty decision: She test-drove only two brands and ended up buying the model she liked more. A few months later, she went to a car show with her husband and saw dozens of makes and models that she hadn't even known existed. Some of them cost less than her new car. She regretted not having thought through all the possibilities, because she could have gotten a better car for her money if she had.

After teaching a second-grade class, a boy told me that when his cousin had come over the previous Saturday, they couldn't think of anything they wanted to do. So they started to complain to his mother. She told them to think of a list of all the different things they could do. And they came up with seven different things: Legos, action figures, forts, basketball, Twister, trading cards, and UNO. After looking at the list, they decided to play Legos. The next time, he says, they'll use their thinking to solve the problem themselves instead of complaining.

A girl told me that she had been in charge of her ninth birthday party, a great exercise in thinking. She had to make a list of the friends and neighbors she wanted to invite, what decorations she wanted, what theme she wanted, what kind of food she wanted, what games she wanted, and what prizes she wanted. She said that she used a lot of thinking and problem solving to come up with as many possibilities as she could, have the party that she wanted, and make sure that her guests had a great time.

## Thinking and Problem Solving Discussion Starters

Thinking and problem solving is a skill that helps both kids and adults in all areas of their lives. Instead of saying they cannot solve a problem and giving up, kids and adults can think of all the possibilities for solutions. We include some ideas for conversations you can have with children about this skill, and you can use your thinking to come up with other conversation topics too.

- When you have a problem that you don't know the answer to, should you give up? Discuss how instead of giving up we need to think of all the possible ways to solve a problem. How does this help at school and home?
- When you are learning new things, should you say you cannot do it? What happens when we always tell ourselves we can't solve problems?
- When are some times you have to use your thinking?
- What is a school subject where thinking and problem solv-

ing would help you improve? Discuss how making a commitment to use thinking and problem solving would help in that area.

## Skill Builders for Adults and Children

- Think of someone you recently saw or heard about who used thinking and problem solving.
- Think of someone you recently saw or heard about who did not use thinking and problem solving. What could the person have done differently?
- Think of a time in the last week when you used your thinking and problem solving.
- When did you not use thinking and problem solving but wish you had? What could you have done differently?
- Have a conversation about role models—people you know who use their thinking to solve problems.
- The skills are everywhere. Give an example of a book, movie, current event, or television show where people or characters either used or didn't their thinking to solve a problem.

## Helpful Hints

Remind children that we all have to use our thinking to solve problems throughout the day. When we do math or science, read, or are challenged by something new, we are using our thinking to solve problems. When you are playing games at recess or at home, you have to use your thinking and problem solving. If you have a problem with a friend, you have to think in order to find a peaceful solution to the problem. You can have children make a list of all the possibilities and pick one to try out. If the solution does not work, they can go back and try out another.

There are other games and activities that you probably have that involve thinking and problem solving. Building blocks and Legos can challenge children's thinking. They use their thinking to envision what they want to make and how they want to make it. Board games such as chess and Scrabble, and even television game shows such as *Jeopardy!* and *Wheel of Fortune* challenge thinking in other ways. Activities such as brain teasers, crossword puzzles, magic tricks, and riddles challenge children to use their creativity. Remind children that all these activities use thinking to solve the problem. They are also great practice for the thinking they will need to use when they solve problems of a personal or academic nature.

Before your children start their homework, you can do a thinking and problem solving activity to help them "warm up" their brains. This will remind them to think of all the possible solutions and be creative in their assignments. Even Boy Scout or Girl Scout leaders (or any other children's club leaders) can play a game like What Else Can This Be? before starting arts-and-crafts activities to help children get ready to think creatively.

Another way to show children how thinking involves many different perspectives is to give them a camera and have them photograph an object from many different angles. This is an interesting way to show kids how there are many different ways to look at things visually, just as there are many different ways to solve problems in everyday life.

Remind children that they are smart as long as they take responsibility to use their brains to think. Continue to remind them that they should never feel stuck. Instead, encourage them to keep thinking until they solve the problem.

~  ~  ~

Using thinking and problem solving is essential not just to a person's individual happiness but also to our entire society. If you face a problem, you can work it out with this skill and find a solution, rather than lashing out in anger and frustration, or sinking into depression and a feeling of worthlessness. This skill can actually help reduce violence in the culture; people who use it find better solutions to tough issues in life. It also helps guide people through life. You can use it to choose a course of study or a life partner, to make decisions about your job and where you want to live, even to decide which candidate to vote for. With it, you can wake up in the morning excited, invigorated, ready to take on the day.

When you use thinking and problem solving, you have an infinite number of possibilities at your fingertips. There is always a new way to look at the situation. You can solve any problem and tackle any challenge.

# 10

# Cooperation

My coauthor watched from his office window as the two planes slammed into the World Trade Center. There is no way to explain away the horror those terrorists perpetrated on the nation and the world. But as news reports of their background, their training, and their motives surfaced, one thing became clear: They had been taught not to listen to other people's voices and not to cooperate with people they considered the "enemy" to find a rational solution to their differences. The only way they could remain effective as terrorists and killers of innocent people was to shut themselves off completely from the idea that two different cultures could cooperate and learn from each other.

This is at the base of every war. While we were writing this book, a newspaper published the obituary of the last suviving man from what came to be known in European history as the Christmas Truce. In 1914, in the freezing, lice-infested, muddy trenches of France, British and German soldiers put down their arms, crawled up into No-Man's-land, and started joking with each other and exchanging food and cigarettes. Soon, they were playing soccer together. They learned that they could play together, which made them recognize one another's humanity. When the truce ended, they crawled back into their trenches.

And they became terrible soldiers.

Both sides soon realized that they had to recall all their men from the front and send in new troops who had never been exposed to each other. The experience of cooperating in staging a Christmas celebration had permanently sapped both British and Germans of any desire to kill one another. Their respective governments took exactly the wrong lesson from the episode. They should have sent the prime minister of England and the kaiser of Germany out to cook a holiday feast together and then play soccer. The war might have ended instantly. Cooperation has just that magical an effect.

Cooperation is a fact of our everyday lives. At work, we usually work on teams or in departments that coordinate everything from job assignments to vacation schedules to make sure that things run smoothly. In our homes, we have to cooperate with our busy schedules when to have dinner, when to go shopping, when to spend time together. Neighbors cooperate—observing boundaries, keeping up their properties, helping one another when in need—in order to make living in close proximity possible. I know one neighborhood whose residents throw a block party every year. Months beforehand, the residents get together and divide up tasks, according to their interests and talents, to make sure that everything goes smoothly on the big day.

And what is a friendship but a form of cooperation? You and your friends decide jointly what you want to do together, where you want to eat, what sports or games you want to play. Often we naturally gravitate toward people with whom we can cooperate.

But cooperation in our society breaks down too often. Sometimes it is badly misunderstood: Kids join gangs and go along with what their leaders tell them to do, from robbing stores and mugging people even to committing murder. They think they are cooperating with a group with a larger purpose when they are actually just being manipulated.

There are less drastic but still worrisome examples. Consider:

Every time we have an election in the United States, we see scores of "attack ads" that have replaced civil discourse and debate in our elections.

More than half of all first marriages end in divorce.

Domestic violence has become one of culture's most pervasive problems. Many people simply don't know any better way to solve disputes.

In prime-time television, reality shows feature contestants who cheat, deceive, and humiliate their own "teammates," and judges who disparage and insult contestants.

The common thread in all these things—a thread that is woven deeply into our culture—is that we often use confrontation instead of cooperation, working for our perceived individual interests instead of the common good.

Not long ago, in a town near where I live, two fathers got into a fight at their sons' hockey game. By the time it ended, one man was dead; the other ended up in prison. As a result, two boys lost their fathers. The incident troubled me not just because of the utterly senseless loss of life, but also because of the example all the children at the rink that day saw: an adult with no self-control committing the worst possible act. The fathers grew up perpetuating the idea that violence is the way to solve problems, and they passed this mentality on to a new generation because they didn't know any other way of life. The need for cooperation in our culture is acute, yet it's not something that our children learn. It has to be.

When cooperation breaks down, it's frequently because our society does not place a premium on the skills we need to cooperate. We may try to resolve conflicts, yet how can we if we don't have the necessary skills to cooperate? If we have not learned the skills in the ABCs of Life, it is nearly impossible to collaborate with others.

Cooperation with your spouse, coworkers, friends, and relatives can be truly challenging. Whether you are decorating your house or agreeing on a family budget, it takes a great deal of self-control to stay calm. It takes self-confidence and responsibility to talk about your feelings and experiences when cooperating regarding politics, religion, or other personal beliefs. Trying your best and thinking are crucial to solving the problems of where to go on vacation or even what movie to see. Like the hockey dads, many of us are more poised for action, even for violence, than for using the skills we need for cooperation. This doesn't mean that resolving conflicts is easy, but self-control, self-confidence, responsibility, and thinking and problem solving are the cornerstone skills for cooperation.

Sometimes the challenge of cooperation is developing creative solutions to the problem. In the children's book *The Phantom Tollbooth* by Norton Juster, the princesses Rhyme and Reason work relentlessly to bring two brothers together. For years, the brothers do not compromise. Through endless trials and tribulations they finally agree to disagree. To avoid chaos, dissonance, or disruption, cooperation sometimes means we also have to agree to disagree.

One of the most exciting moments in a Lesson One program

at any school is the day when we discuss cooperation. This is the culmination of the skills. It requires students to use their listening skill to hear what everyone is saying, to treat others the way they would like to be treated, to celebrate the diversity of the people with whom they are working; to respect their varied opinions, to try their best to work together; to use self-control (or take a Self-Control Time) so that they don't fight with others, to have the self-confidence to stand up for what they believe in, to take responsibility and make things happen or not happen, and to use thinking and problem solving to come up with all the possible solutions they can in any situation. Everything we have discussed, from the Pledge for Success onward, comes together here. Cooperation is a skill that children can learn at an early age and use throughout their lives. We all need to use cooperation daily.

*Cooperation is when I work well with others. I cooperate to solve problems and resolve conflicts.*

In today's world, we interact with things more than we do with people. The way kids learn to play nowadays often does little to teach cooperation. Watching television together and playing video games in pairs don't allow kids to interact with one another; the children are interacting only with technology.

When kids do play together, adults always tell them to play nice or cooperate when playing with others, but efforts to demonstrate how this can be done are few and far between. To foster this practice, we ask children to get into huddles. Huddles provide a positive structure for interactions.

This is not like a football huddle. Instead, children stand face-to-face with their hands at their sides so that they're comfortable in their own space as they cooperate. Our huddles are more like the kind of conversation you and a partner might have at home about what to have for dinner, or you and a colleague might have in the office or around the watercooler about how to proceed on a project. They're the kind of cooperative conversation we all have every day—or that we all should have. We use huddles to play the Huddle game.

In a classroom setting, we ask the teacher's help to put together two or more kids who don't usually work together. Kids with varied interests, kids of diverse backgrounds and cultures, are joined together in these huddles to help them understand that their similarities far outweigh their differences and that they can work with anyone toward common goals. This can be useful in discouraging schoolyard bullying; it's hard to bully another kid you've worked with successfully. In this exercise, children can see each other as people, not stereotypes or objects of scorn. As always, when we introduce huddles, we remind kids the series of sequential skills they have learned up to this point.

Monitor the huddles the kids form; if necessary, remind them that cooperation is not about bullying or bossing your partner into agreement. One person cannot pick the answer; it's important that everyone agrees. Likewise, don't let kids simply shrug and say "whatever," as if their opinions don't matter or, worse, they don't care. Cooperation builds on responsibility: Every person is responsible for adding an honest opinion to the mix.

We've seen kids in huddles who simply stand silent. Often that's because they let others in the huddle intimidate them into keeping their opinions unvoiced. They let someone else become the bully and they allow themselves to become the victim. But if they speak up for themselves, then the bully doesn't have a victim to overpower. We remind huddle participants that they need to use the ABCs of Life when they deal with bullies in a huddle. We tell them that it takes self-confidence to stand up for their beliefs, and it takes responsibility to stand up for themselves.

When you have introduced kids to the concept of working together in pairs, start them in groups of three, then move to even bigger groups. You can ask them more serious questions. A very constructive way to teach cooperation is to tell children to imagine that they have just been given a magic lamp. A genie will emerge and grant them one wish. But it can't be anything selfish; the wish has to be something that will better the entire world. The kids can cooperate to decide what is the best thing they can ask for—eradicating hunger, or famine, or war, for example.

This kind of question does more than just teach children how to cooperate with one another. They're pretty quick to pick up on the idea that they can agree on a movie or a lunch. It broadens the concept into the culture as a whole, reminding them that they have to work together to solve some of our society's ills. At an early age, they begin to understand that, through cooperation, they can change the world.

The Huddle Game is a practical and useful tool for cooperation. You can use huddles whenever there is a problem at home or in the classroom. When children understand how huddles work, they can use them as a tool to help them cooperate to solve their problems. They can use huddles if they're having trouble deciding what game to play, working on a group project, having a problem with a classmate, making choices as a class, or deciding what movie to see. For example, rather than kids fighting over what they want to do (what TV show to watch, what game to play), kids could form huddles to help solve the problems and use their thinking to think of all the possibilities.

When Mimi and I were engaged to be married, we both had ideas about the possible style and theme of the wedding. Mimi wanted a romantic, outdoor event with champagne, strawberries, folk songs, a harp, and a flute. I wanted more of a variety show–type extravaganza. I hoped to have a barbershop quartet, a belly dancer for my Uncle Leon, and I wanted to walk down the aisle to "Chim-Chim-Cheree" while performing magic tricks. After several discussions, we decided to compromise—we pulled off a romantic, vaudeville wedding. Everybody, including us, had a great time. No two people ever have identical tastes; by compromising, Mimi and I set the scene for cooperation in the later years of our marriage.

Mimi is a clinical social worker and also practices holistic massage and bodywork therapies. A few years ago, she began seeing clients at our house. But there was one problem. I love clocks and gadgets of all kinds. I have cuckoo clocks, grandfather clocks, musical clocks, and phones—all of which make noise and play music. When Mimi started seeing clients, the noise from these things ruined the relaxed and focused atmosphere of the house. So we had to cooperate. We decided that I could still have my clocks, as long as they had an On/Off switch. That way, Mimi can turn off my clocks when she is giving a massage. And when I come home, I can turn them back on. By cooperating, we arrived at a conclusion that benefited us both.

Define cooperation for the kids while you're teaching it. Tell them that cooperation means working well with others. Whether they're playing jump rope or football, it's a way to solve problems and resolve conflicts at home and at school. It's something that adults do too. It's a skill they will be able to use for their whole lives, and they can cooperate with anyone. For that reason, it's important that you make sure that kids do their huddles with different people every time; they should grow comfortable with dealing with kids and adults of varied backgrounds.

Jackie Robinson was not accepted by many of his Brooklyn Dodgers teammates. Perhaps the greatest story in baseball history involved the white shortstop Pee Wee Reese. When he was sent to serve in the South Pacific during World War II, 10,000 fans signed a petition demanding that Reese be replaced by a shortstop from the Negro League. It didn't happen, but Dodger fans naturally assumed that Reese, hurt and angry when he came back from combat, would resent Robinson, who in 1947 became the first African-American Major League player. Instead, when fans booed Robinson on the field, Reese made a point of very publicly walking over to his new teammate and wrapping an arm around him. He was respecting diversity, of course, but he was also teaching a lesson in the importance of cooperation.

When you talk about cooperation with kids, you can give them real-life examples. For example, on a football team, a quarterback still throws to the receiver, even if they're not best friends. All the teachers in a school may not see eye to eye, but they still cooperate to make the school work smoothly. All of the members of a community may not be close, but they cooperate too, whether over a community garden, a celebration, or a new building plan. Cooperation means getting the job done, thinking, planning, and working together. Age, race, or gender does not matter when you're cooperating. We can all work together while respecting diversity.

You can talk about subjects like the United Nations, a place where people of all backgrounds, races, ethnicities, and colors come together to try to make the world better through cooperation. "I don't know how many wars have been avoided because people could come here and talk to each other," says veteran

U.N. worker Betty Teslenko. From negotiating the end of the blockade of Berlin in the 1940s to helping avert wars in Haiti and the Middle East in the current age, the U.N. has used cooperation on a global scale to achieve positive results for all parties. In a sense, we live in a global playground, where bullies and weaker kids are represented by aggressive nations and smaller ones. The ABCs of Life apply on a global scale as much as they do on a local one. Like a teacher or a parent, the United Nations can't always avert conflict because too many people and nations still do not understand cooperation. When nations cooperate, the world becomes a better place. And we have to keep trying to apply the skills across the world.

It's our responsibility as adults to serve as models for cooperation, which reminds me of a story that would be funny if it weren't actually sad. I was in a school once where I decided it might be an interesting exercise to combine third- and fourth-grade classes in a cooperation exercise. These children normally were not in class with each other; many of them did not know each other. I thought it would help break down barriers and teach them that they could get along with and cooperate even with any members of the school.

I sought the cooperation of the teachers in each class for my idea. They agreed that it might be a marvelous exercise. But they imposed one condition: They wouldn't both be in the same classroom at the same time. It turned out that they couldn't stand each other. What kind of models were they for the children in their charge?

As the adults in our families, we can be good models for kids. When children see us working together to decide what to plant in a garden, where to go on a vacation, what to eat for dinner, they learn the value of cooperation. Whether or not you use the term "huddle" formally to refer to these transactions, you are showing children the importance of cooperation. If a child sees adults come together to discuss where they live, what they buy, and how they spend their time together, the example is far more valuable than any number of lectures.

One way we teach this lesson is by playing the Sketch To-gether game, using that old standby the Etch-A-Sketch. If you haven't used one in a while, you many not know that this toy now comes in a small, almost palm-sized model. You can play this game with your child, or if you're playing in a large group, ask as many adults as there are available to sit next to children, then pair off the remaining kids.

We ask two people to share one Etch-A-Sketch. Each person handles only the knob nearest to him or her. One knob controls the vertical; the other, the horizontal. Each pair cooperates to produce an image.

Start by suggesting simple shapes—boxes, numbers, letters—that kids might make together. Then, when they have success-fully completed a few designs, ask them to come up with other images on their own. They can discuss and agree on what they want to draw—a house, a computer, or a tree, for example—and work together to draft the contours of the drawing.

As they design things together, kids start using all the skills, as well as the elements of the Pledge for Success. They learn that they have diverse talents and ideas, and that diversity doesn't keep them from cooperating. They use their self-confidence to suggest ideas and advocate for themselves, their self-control not to fight, and their listening so they can hear what others have to say. Collectively, they take responsibility for getting the job done.

I had an example of this in my own childhood. When Mark and I were kids, we played alone a lot together, often with an

Erector Set we had. (For people who don't remember them, Erector Sets had tiny metal beams, girders, bolts, nuts, and screws, which encouraged kids to use their imaginations to build skyscrapers, helicopters, roller coasters, and virtually anything else they could think of.)

Mark, the future doctor, had manual dexterity coming out his ears; I remember that he built a parachute jump once. Probably some of his inventions were precursors of the first heart-lung machine or the first space shuttle. I was, shall we say, differently talented. One day when I designed a project, I simply picked up one piece of metal and held it up, moving it through the air all around the room and announced, "Look, I made a magic carpet to fly around the parachute jump." Mark celebrated my simple invention as happily as I acknowledged his intricate work. We worked together with that toy for months, cooperating every time, supporting each other with our diversity of interests, talents, and imagination.

Another thing that my brother and I did was play with the trains that Effie's boyfriend, Sid, gave us. We sat together every Saturday, setting them up, taking them apart, constructing ornate and complicated railroads. This indelible memory of our cooperation made such an impact on me that today I have a little room in my house that is devoted to my set of trains. My favorites are the handcars. I love the fact that in order to move, the train must be driven by two figures, one who pushes up and one who pushes down. Watching these trains go reminds me of the give-and-take of cooperating with Mark, and the other aspects of cooperation that we all deal with every day.

Our culture—indeed, the entire world—needs to learn cooperation. Over lunch one day, Michael Ryan told me about a trip he

took to Mali, one of the poorest countries in the world, watching
the ubiquitous white-and-blue trucks of the United Nations delivering food and medicines to people in need, and seeing U.N.
trucks bringing potable water to Cambodian refugees in South-
east Asia. What's striking about these missions is that they are
staffed by people from every continent (except Antarctica; penguins can't drive). Let children know that co-operation is essential for a culture to thrive and prosper, and show them early on
how important cooperation is in their own lives.

In recent years, there have been significant advances in the
treatment of AIDS. That happened because scientists working
on the problem come together every year at a global meeting and share their information. No vaccine has been found, but
they discovered that, by combining the drugs they had discovered, they could lengthen people's lives. Neighborhoods
around the country have cut crime and improved their quality
of life by setting up neighborhood watches, in which people,
working together, observe and report crimes and suspicious
activities.

If cooperation were embedded in the daily routine of life, we
would be able to deal with things before they happen, as op-
posed to cleaning up after the damage is done. Imagine if, when
conflicts occur, people started dealing with each other by using
the skills, rather than by fighting and waging war. What a peaceful world it would be.

## Teaching the ABCs of Life:
## Cooperation

### 1: INTRODUCE AND DEFINE IT

Cooperation

Cooperation is when I work well with others. I cooperate to solve problems and resolve conflicts.

After cutting out the cooperation poster in the Appendix, read the definition aloud together and introduce cooperation to your child. Here are some suggestions.

"Cooperation is working well with other people to solve problems. When we cooperate, we use all of the skills. We listen to each other, respect the diversity of other people's opinions, treat others the way we'd like to be treated, try our best, use our self-control, have the self-confidence to say how we feel, take responsibility for our actions, and use our thinking to think of all of the possibilities and solve problems. I cooperate to solve problems when I am at home and work. We cooperate when we want to watch different shows on television. Instead of fighting, we cooperate to decide on a show we both enjoy watching. When I am at work and I work on a project with other people, we cooperate to solve problems, just as you cooperate to solve problems when you're at school and you work on a project with a group of classmates. When we cooperate, we can have fun instead of arguing and we share our feelings in a peaceful way."

## 2: EXPERIENCE IT

### Huddle Games

Have you ever had to work closely with another person to solve a problem? Sometimes it can be quite a challenge. This game helps children learn that it takes all of the skills to cooperate with others.

1. Before the game, discuss with the children the skills we all need to cooperate. It takes self-control to treat others the way you would like to be treated while cooperating. You have to listen and try not to boss people. You also have to have self-confidence to stand up for your own ideas. You have to take responsibility for yourself and think of the great variety of ways you can solve the problem.

2. Let the children know that we are going to work together to learn an interesting way to cooperate. It is called a huddle. Explain that a huddle is when two or more people face each other to solve problems and cooperate.

3. Begin by showing the children what a huddle looks like. Choose someone to be your huddle partner. Explain that the first step to a huddle is facing your partner in your own

space. Also explain that it's important to stand with self-confidence with your arms at your side. When your arms are crossed, this makes your body tight.

4. If there are enough children, divide them into pairs. You can also be in a pair to show that adults need to cooperate just like kids do.

5. Ask children a concrete question that they can cooperate to solve. Here's an example: You and your partner are in an ice cream store and you have enough money for only one scoop of ice cream. Together you have to decide what is the one flavor that you will both share. (For older children, you can say that the store does not have vanilla, chocolate, or strawberry; this helps spur their imagination.)

6. Remind the children to respect each other's opinions and to think creatively to solve the problem.

7. At the end of the session, ask the members of each huddle to share their answers with everyone else.

8. Reinforce the lesson by telling the children that they are doing a great job at cooperation. Then give them another problem to solve. Here's a sample: You and your friend are going out to lunch. Unfortunately, you have enough money for only one meal and one beverage. Together, you have to decide what you will share for lunch and for your drink. When the waiter comes over to the table, he tells you that the restaurant is out of pizza, hamburgers, and chicken fingers. Cooperate and use your thinking to solve the problem.

9. Give the children a chance to come up with huddle problems as well.

FURTHER SUGGESTIONS

- If you are playing this game in the classroom or in a large group, have children form huddles with people they do not usually work or play with.

After playing the game, discuss the following questions:

- What skills did you have to use to cooperate with someone else?
- Do you sometimes have to compromise or not always get your first choice when you cooperate?

## Huddle Games of Three or More

Tell the kids that, as an adult, you know from experience that it's hard to work in a group of two people, let alone a group of three or more. Then introduce them to larger huddles. This game helps children to learn to use the skill of cooperation in larger groups.

1. Have the children divide into a huddle of three or more or get into a huddle as a family.
2. Discuss the fact that when we work in larger groups we have to use a great deal of self-control to listen to everybody (because there are more ideas in larger groups). Remind children that it takes self-control not to be bossy, self-confidence to stand up for what you believe in, and a lot of thinking and cooperation to find something that everyone can agree on.
3. Begin by asking the huddle about a concrete problem that the members can cooperate to solve. Here's an example: You and your partners are together on a Saturday after-

noon. What is one thing that you would like to do to-gether? (For older children, you can say that they do not have a television, video games, or a bike.)

4. Have the children in huddles share their answers.

5. If you haven't already participated in a huddle, join one so that kids and adults can cooperate to solve a problem to-gether.

6. Think of another question to ask the huddle. Below are some ideas.

    • You and your partners found a magic lamp. With this magic lamp you get to make one wish. The wish has to be something that will make the world a better place. The magic lamp will not give you money. Cooperate to decide what your one wish will be.

    • Cooperate to decide on one thing that will make your school a better place for everyone. Remember that school is a place for learning.

7. Huddle questions and situations can cover all aspects of life. The following huddle questions can help children have a point of reference for how to cooperate in difficult situations. Once children know what huddles are, you can ask the questions in huddles of two or in huddles of three or more. You can also feel free to brainstorm age-appropriate topics.

    • You and your friends saw a classmate steal something from someone's locker. In a huddle, cooperate to decide what to do about this problem.

    • One of your friends has started taking drugs. In your huddles, please cooperate to think of all the ways that you can help your friend.

After playing the game, ask the following questions:

- What skills did you have to use to cooperate with a group of people?
- Was it more challenging to work with three or more people? Why?
- What are some times when you can use huddles at home, at school, or in the neighborhood?

If children don't come up with answers, help them a bit. Remind them that thinking and problem solving, self-confidence and responsibility, as well as self-control, all come into play in cooperation. They'll probably tell you that it's harder to work with more people, because more varied opinions must be taken into account and respected; if they don't, ask them about it. If they can't come up with ideas about how to use huddles at home, prime the pump a little. Suggest they might think about what to watch on television, or what game to play, and ask them to come up with other examples.

## Sketch Together

Have you ever had a difficult time working with someone else? Talk about it. Explain that sometimes it's not easy to cooperate. Cooperating with someone else is a challenge. But children need to learn that the skill of cooperation can be applied throughout their lives.

1. Let the children know that they will be playing a game with you or someone else, and remind them that cooperation means that they are able to work with anyone.
2. Ask the children (and adults) to get in huddles of two and give each group an Etch-A-Sketch. Have everyone find a

seat. You can work with a partner too, so that children see how important it is for adults to cooperate.

3. Explain that each person is allowed to touch only one Etch-A-Sketch knob (the knob closest to him or her).

4. Give the players a concrete object to create. They can start by drawing a box together. Remind the players that it takes self-control to touch only their knobs and that they can cooperate by talking together about who needs to move his or her knob. Allow them two minutes to make a box. Remind them that it is okay to make mistakes and to have fun cooperating with each other.

5. After the task is done, have each pair cooperate to decide who is going to shake the Etch-A-Sketch. They can take turns, shake it together, or use any other method they decide on.

6. Next, have the pairs cooperate to make another object. Capital letters work very well—you can try simple geometric shapes like L, T, and H, and, if the children are ready for the challenge, D and O.

7. To reinforce the skill, between each activity remind the partners to cooperate to decide who is going to shake the Etch-A-Sketch.

8. Give children a chance to come up with objects to design too.

FURTHER SUGGESTIONS

- If you are playing this game in the classroom or with a large group of kids, tell the children that they have to use their self-control to not touch the Etch-A-Sketch until you give the directions. The consequence of using self-control is being able to play the game. The consequence of not using self-control is having the Etch-A-Sketch taken away. Emphasize that the children can get the Etch-A-Sketch back once they get their self-control back. If this happens, be sure to congratulate the child for getting her self-control back by telling her she should be proud of herself.

- For some variety, while in huddles, have the children decide which one of them is Player A and which one is Player B. Then say, "Player A, go," and after a few seconds say, "Player A, stop." During that time, Player A should be moving the knob to make a design. Then do the same thing for Player B. Repeat this process several times. You can also have both players turn the knob at the same time. Then challenge the children to use their cooperation and thinking and problem-solving skills to decide and then share what their pictures look like. The idea is to cooperate and come up with one answer together.

After playing the game, ask the following questions:

- What skills did you use to cooperate with your partner?
- When are some times you both need to cooperate?

Have a discussion about how cooperation requires that you use your self-control to treat others the way you would like to be treated. It's important to learn to listen and not boss people around. You also have to have self-confidence to stand up for your ideas. You have to take responsibility for yourself and think of all the different ways to solve the problem.

## 3: *SHARE IT*
### Share Stories About Cooperation

As you begin to think about sharing from your own life, here are some anecdotes that friends, colleagues, and people from around the country have shared with me. Please share these stories and your own stories about cooperation, and ask kids to share their stories about cooperation too.

Last summer, one of my coworkers went on vacation with her boyfriend. The couple has very different tastes: While my coworker's favorite vacation activity is relaxing on the beach, her boyfriend enjoys hiking in the woods. Instead of choosing just one of these options, they decided to cooperate and find someplace that offered both. First, they had a conversation about all the options they had. After listening to each other and thinking of all their possibilities, they decided to see if they could find someplace near the water that offered hiking as well. So they took the responsibility to do some research together and, sure enough, they found a campsite that offered oceanside camping and hiking trails through the forest. The campsite's several hiking trails led them to beautiful white-sand beaches. Due to their successful cooperation, both of them ended up having a great time, despite the mosquitoes. Next time, they'll bring a lot more bug spray.

A nurse I know works in an emergency room. On Friday nights, the hospital gets very busy. Everyone works together to decide on where to put all the patients and how to prioritize them. Without cooperation, the patients wouldn't get the care that they need.

One boy told me about how he and his friend who lived down the street used to argue all the time. His friend had a big slide in his backyard, and the boy who told me the story had a playroom in his house. Every day, they squabbled over whose house they would go to after school. Some days, they didn't play together, because they couldn't decide. The boy said that his mother told them that they needed to cooperate to solve their problem. So they formed a huddle and decided that on nice days, they would go to his friend's house, where the slide is, and play outside. On rainy or cold days, they would go to his house to use the playroom. And then on days that could go either way, they decided to split up the time they spent at both houses, so that they didn't go to one house more than the other.

A seventh-grade girl told me about a team science project that her teacher had assigned in the beginning of the school year. She was paired up with a girl who was pretty bossy, while she was very shy. Since her partner liked to make decisions, the girl let her. She didn't take any responsibility and also let her partner do the thinking and problem solving that the project required. But at the end of the project, her partner was angry that the girl hadn't done her share, and the girl herself didn't like the way the project turned out, either. A few months later, they were paired again. This time, she said, they worked together and made decisions as a team, and in the end, they both felt a lot better about the finished product because they had cooperated.

## Cooperation Discussion Starters

Imagine what a different world we would live in if we all knew how to cooperate. By talking with your children about cooperation, you not only help them to further internalize the skill, but to also better understand how much kids and adults both need to cooperate.

- On a baseball team, are all the players best friends, or do they learn to work together? Are all the teachers in a school best friends, or all the students in a classroom? Do members of the United Nations have to join to cooperate with one another? Explain that we all have to work together. You won't always get a chance to work with your best friend. You have to be able to cooperate with anyone.
- Discuss how it can be challenging to cooperate with groups of people. What are some times you will have to cooperate with three or more people?
- How can you use cooperation at home and school?
- How is self-control important when you cooperate?
- What should you do if you get stuck solving a problem?
- What happens when one person in the huddle is bossing everyone else around? (You need to take responsibility to speak up for yourself and use your self-control.)
- What should you do if you feel shy and intimidated by other people in the huddle? (speak with self-confidence)
- If someone else is not sharing their ideas, how can you help that person? (treat him or her the way you want to be treated and ask how he or she feels)
- Is there somebody in your class or neighborhood you have a hard time cooperating with? What can you do over the next few days to help you get along better?

## Skill Builders for Adults and Children

- Think of people you recently saw or heard about who co-operated.
- Think of people you recently saw or heard about who did not cooperate. What could they have done differently?
- Think of a time in the last week when you cooperated with others.
- When did you not use cooperation but wish you had? What could you have done differently?
- Have a conversation about role models—people you know—who cooperate well with others.
- The skills are everywhere. Give an example of a book, movie, current event, or television show where people or characters either did or did not cooperate with others.

## Helpful Hints

Huddles can naturally become a part of everyday life. In the classroom, form huddles when you ask questions related to school subjects such as math or history and have the kids work together to solve the problem. When working on group projects, whether it's an art project or science, have the kids form huddles so they can work together in deciding what their project is going to be, how they're going to do it, and who's going to do what. It takes all of the skills to cooperate with each other. To further this exercise, pair together groups who don't normally work together so that everyone can have a chance to respect diversity.

During team games like soccer or basketball and baseball, remind the players that these activities require that everyone works together with cooperation. In life, we all have to learn to cooperate with others, no matter who they may be.

If your child is sitting around on a Saturday complaining that he is bored, remind him that the person who's making him bored is himself. Form a huddle together and think of all the possibilities of what he can do. Or if your child has a friend over and they begin arguing over what they want to do, have them form a huddle and remind them that they need to listen to each other, respect each other's diversity, and use their thinking to think of all the different things they can do together.

If two children have a disagreement over a toy, then you can ask them to get into a huddle and cooperate to solve the problem. Huddles can be particularly helpful in solving disputes that may occur between friends. If one child discovers that another child has been talking about him behind his back, instead of fighting back with words or fists, children can form a huddle to solve the problem instead of perpetuating it.

In a family, huddles are very helpful in deciding what movie you want to rent, what music to listen to in the car, where you want to go on family vacation, what board game you want to play together—any decision you make together as a family. Forming a huddle allows everyone to listen to each other, speak up with self-confidence, and think of all the different possibilities together. When we cooperate, we often have to comprimse to reach a decision together. Remind young children that cooperation is not about winning or losing but about finding a solution to a problem that everyone agrees on.

~ ~ ~

It takes all the skills to cooperate. I can imagine a world in which all children learn it, along with all the other skills. Lesson One is not a panacea, but it is the first step toward achieving a future with less war, fewer crimes, and less violence. We would have a culture that supports, rather than exploits. It would make each of us happier.

Is it impossible to achieve? No, it's not impossible. Is it a utopian vision? No, it can happen. Will it be easy? Cultures are hard to change; we have to move them one person at a time. Still, to quote Charles Darwin, "There is a grandeur in this view of life."

# 11

# Putting It Together

It's hard for any of us to ignore the terrorism, shootings, and random acts of violence that help destroy our culture every day. When I see such atrocities, I feel for the victims. But in a strange way, I also feel sorrow for the perpetrators. Of course, I don't condone their acts, but I constantly wonder what happened in their lives that made them commit such acts. Weren't they once children? The Unabomber, the Columbine shooters, the snipers who terrorized the Washington area—all had intelligence, education, opportunities, advantages.

What went wrong?

Most people who commit horrible acts started out as regular kids. Any one of them might have been the baby in the crib next to your own son or daughter in the maternity ward. If only, somewhere in their early lives, they had learned the skills that they needed to survive and succeed in their lives, perhaps things would have turned out differently for them and their victims.

In 1967, I saw the film adaptation of Truman Capote's book *In Cold Blood*. The film's main characters slaughtered an entire Kansas farm family, mistakenly believing that the father kept large amounts of cash in the farmhouse. With no remorse, they killed not only the farmer but also his wife and two young children.

When my parents saw the film, they were, like most people, horrified. I asked them why they were so astonished by the violent nature of the grown-up killer and reminded them of a chilling flashback scene from the childhood of one of the murderers: The killer's father angrily threatened him with a gun when he was still a child. Twenty years later, he was doing the same thing to other innocent people. While it's no excuse for what he did, I thought that the killer was only perpetuating what he had experienced in his early life. My parents didn't understand what I was talking about.

When I reflect on this experience and the feelings I had then and still feel, I always think of that day in a second-grade classroom when a little girl uttered the heartbreaking words, "My father held a gun to me. My parents are getting divorced."

This is reality.

This kind of event is not something that happens only in the movies. Violence and fear are prevalent in our rapidly disintegrating culture, and this little girl's words speak for generations past and many generations yet to come. It's important that all of us take heed. If we do not take these skills in, internalize them, and pass them on to today's children, we are burying them alive. We watch the news, we read the newspapers. We see the violence firsthand. How can we *not* give children these skills? The skills are the life preservers we can cling to in the tumultuous sea of life.

As I emphasize throughout this book, teaching the skills is a mission for parents and teachers. This mission is important for anyone who works or lives with kids, or for anyone who cares about the future of our society. Consider the support that I found in my life: Mr. Dupee during my school days, Joe Kruger at summer camp, Mrs. Simonds through my college years. I had my grandmother, Aunt Fran, and Uncle Leon. And most of all, I had Effie. She provided me with the foundation of skills on which all of the others whom I have mentioned built.

After Effie died, I felt isolated. But then I began to reflect on all that she had left with me. She gave me the skills, and these skills changed my life. As long as I had the skills, I realized, I would never be alone. It was comforting to know that I would always have the skills to fall back on. I had myself, and the confidence, self-control, and other skills that told me I could depend on myself. For over thirty years, it has been my mission to pass these skills along to as many children as I can, to give them the skills that Effie and others gave me.

Two months after Effie's death, I met Mimi, who, like Effie, has provided me with unconditional love. She's been my wife for more than twenty years now. In our relationship, as well as with friends, at work, and in schools with teachers and children alike, I am constantly amazed at the fun, exhilarating process of the skills. I continually experience growth in the ups and downs of this rewarding, yet challenging adventure called life. I've come to realize that the skills are for everyone, both adults and children, everywhere in the world.

I have shared Lesson One with as many people as possible; it is my hope that they in turn do the same. I have realized that Lesson One can be a worldwide program. I have dedicated my life to spreading Lesson One's mission to one school at a time, one class at a time, ultimately to one child at a time, starting with my son.

~ ~ ~

Mimi and I took a vacation at Disney World to celebrate our tenth anniversary. On the day we returned home, I received a phone call from an adoption agency, asking whether we would be willing to adopt a four-day-old baby boy. The only catch was that we had to pick him up the next day. I wanted to jump at the opportunity, but I was alone at home. After Mimi returned, we decided together that we would adopt Andy. We brought him home the next day, exactly ten years to the day after Mimi and I were married.

The joy that I felt about this decision grew every time I held Andy. However, this was a joy marked by sorrow. While holding him made me indescribably happy, I couldn't believe that my parents had never held me. I loved reading to him and putting him to bed. I wondered why my parents had never read to me, why I had to put myself to bed. I felt a void in my life.

But I learned not to blame my parents for this void. Although they were not great parents, I know that they loved me in their own way. My father was only imitating the behavior he thought was expected of a doctor, and as a result, he placed himself on a pedestal. My mother repeated habits that she had seen growing up, and she was at a social disadvantage after skipping five grades. Effie was the person who loved me unconditionally and supported me throughout my childhood. Some people don't have that unconditional love in their lives. But if they have the skills, they can overcome the voids that dysfunction leaves. And if they have the skills early in their lives, they can counter the negative effects of their upbringings and learn to love themselves.

In the movie *The Lion King*, Simba's life becomes chaotic,

with his father dead and his murderous uncle threatening to take Simba's life and take over the throne vacated by Simba's father's death. Instead of becoming stuck in this quagmire, Simba takes action and takes responsibility. He saves his life, his family, his kingdom. We all must take control of the circumstances that we are dealt in our lives, just as Simba did. We must incorporate the skills into our lives and our children's lives so that we can all overcome any obstacles that stand in our way.

When my mother died, I realized that I needed to take responsibility to ask my father to tell me that he loved me. And when he did, he whispered it so softly that I could barely hear him. That was enough for me. I had finally realized that I could not sit around waiting for my father to fill my expectations. I had figured out how to take responsibility for myself. Giving myself what I needed was up to no one but me. So instead of waiting around to see if my father would buy something for Andy's birthday, I took responsibility and brought him to Toys 'R' Us and asked him to buy the portable crib that Andy needed. And so my father bought Andy a portable crib.

As I have traveled around the country with Lesson One, I have achieved a marriage between my personal and professional lives. I have received feedback about the skills and I have shared stories and listened to stories. Everything that I learn and everything that I internalize, I share with my son and children throughout the country in order to help them take charge of their lives.

Growing up with Effie made me feel biracial, and this helped me to perceive how Andy would feel in his life experiences as a biracial child. I knew that it was important to surround him with friends that were family and family that were friends. At a celebration for Andy's arrival, my friend "Grandma Costella" read him the book *The Runaway Bunny* by Margaret Wise Brown, which speaks to the idea of unconditional love. In the book, the mother bunny states that she will always love and be there for her son, no matter where he strays. Just as the Pledge for Success says, families are made up of people who care about you no matter what; in return, you care about them.

When Andy was in kindergarten, his teacher asked the children to draw a picture that would tell the rest of the class about themselves. Underneath his picture, Andy told the teacher to write, "The best thing about me is that I am never alone." I was heartened that Andy really internalized the idea of family and unconditional love.

While we are happy that Andy feels this way, it is equally important for him to know that he always has the skills to fall back on. With the ABCs of Life he will never be alone because he will always get what he needs from himself. Other people can help him and provide him with a consistent environment, but it is ultimately up to him to love himself and make his life his own.

Together, we're constantly finding moments to talk about the skills. Once, Andy and I went to an arcade. Next to us, a father and his daughter were playing a soccer game. The challenge of the game was to kick the soccer ball into a target. As the girl continued to miss the target, her father carried on yelling at her, telling her what a failure she was. Eventually the girl became so frustrated that she quit playing the game.

After we finished at the arcade, Andy and I went on a bus ride. Andy asked to switch seats so that he could sit across from me because he had some things to talk about.

"Why does he have to do that to her?" he asked. "Why can't he just understand that she's trying her best?"

Andy and I talked about what a difference the ABCs of Life

would make in the lives of these two people. If the father had the skills, he could congratulate his daughter on trying her best instead of berating her. And if the daughter had the skills, she'd have the self-confidence to continue playing instead of giving up because she knew that she was trying her best.

"Why can't we all treat others the way that we would like to be treated?" he asked.

Andy continued to ask the questions we all do: Why? Why can't we celebrate the diversity of others? Why is there war? Why is killing an acceptable answer?

We talked about *The Iron Giant*. In the movie, war tears the world apart, and a colossal robot becomes the most effective killing machine in history. One child takes responsibility to go against the entire military-industrial complex and teaches the Iron Giant the futility of war. Peace, to the consternation of the generals, breaks out.

Andy admitted that the idea of war scared him. On his own, he suggested that watching a scary movie might help him to overcome his fears. Shortly thereafter, we both watched *Abbott and Costello Meet Frankenstein*. Watching the comedy/horror movie was a way for Andy to work out his fears that were on a much higher level. I was amazed that Andy had taken responsibility for himself and tried to think of a personal solution to a frightening problem.

After this incident, I continued to wonder: What if? What would happen if everyone had the ABCs of Life?

We all have voids in our lives; these voids don't disappear. Perhaps your family had problems with violence or abuse, your parents may have been divorced, or you may have even been overprotected. For some, there may have been few problems, but still, you may never have been taught skills that empower you in your life. Families pass down wonderful things, but in addition, dysfunction gets passed along from generation to generation. This is not an area to place blame: People often just repeat what they learned from their parents. But for the first time, Lesson One helps you define, experience, and share the skills so you can break the cycle and take charge of your life from a new, exciting, and challenging perspective.

*So close your eyes on Hush-a-Bye Mountain*
*Wave goodbye to cares of the day*

I love this Sherman Brothers lullaby because it reminds me that we can begin each day anew. When Andy was young, I used to sing this to him before he went to bed. Although I wish that someone had done this for me, I accept that it didn't happen and still sing it to myself often. I know I'm lucky—I found the people in my life who shared the skills with me, and I've passed them on to my son. Now Andy is armed with the optimism, hope, and romanticized version of life that my beloved musicals provide. But more important, from the day he was born, Andy has been internalizing the ABCs of Life to prepare him to deal with the realities and challenges of today and tomorrow.

It's up to us to use the skills and figure out what we want to do with our lives instead of lamenting our present circumstances. It's up to us to take the skills and use them in our lives: to follow the Pledge for Success by celebrating diversity and trying our best and treating others the way that we'd like to be treated, to use our self-control, to realize that we are the only ones who can give ourselves self-confidence, to take responsibility to help ourselves and give ourselves what we need, to use our thinking to solve all sorts of problems, to cooperate with anyone. The skills are adaptable to your individual situations and needs. No matter what challenge you may come across in your life, you can refer to the skills and use them to help you decide the direction in which you want your life to go.

I did this. I took the skills of Lesson One and I applied them to my own life. Then I brought them into Andy's life and have been trying to introduce them into the lives of countless children and adults throughout the country. You don't have to meet thousands of people, but you can help change the lives of children and adults around you by teaching them the skills. They work for everybody; the skills transcend age, gender, socioeconomic class, and location. Life is not always smooth sailing. It's a series of ups and downs. The ABCs of Life are not a panacea— they are a continuous process of living. The ABCs of Life are about having a point of reference to go back to, learning from our mistakes and new experiences, and making our life our own. Learning the skills is as important as learning the alphabet and numbers. They are the foundation on which real life is based.

It's vital that the ABCs of Life reach all children. There is a small percentage of children who are hiding behind blank expressions, but underneath their empty façades lies a lifetime of pain. These children have been bullied on the playground, or physically abused, or mentally scarred to the point that they are a danger to themselves and others. These are children who, without warning, might grab a gun and start shooting, plant an explosive, or erupt in a deadly, smoldering, and unforeseen rage. Some children are like time bombs, and we don't know when they'll go off. We never know exactly who they are, either.

For the safety of our future, it's so important to reach children at a young age so that they can internalize the skills. That way, they can overcome whatever hand they've been dealt in life. These threats confront a minority of children, but these threats are real, and these children need to be reached. Innocent lives are at stake, including their own. Imagine the impact you can make on all children. Imagine what could happen if you touched the life of a child. You could help a child transform his or her life and make a difference in our culture.

After reading this book, after bringing these skills into your own life, share them with others. You might be the only person in a child's life. By giving these skills to children, you can help them to take ownership of them, internalize them, and use them forever. After you've done that, pass the book along so that another adult can use the skills and pass them on to another child. Our whole culture can break cycles of dysfunction, violence, and mistrust that have been passed down through generations. All children can grow up knowing that their life is their own. Helping one child at a time, together, we can change the culture of our world and give children what has been missing in their lives: Lesson One.

# APPENDIX

# LESSON ONE GUIDE
# THE ABCs OF LIFE
# SEQUENCING THE SKILLS

* **Pledge for Success:** The Pledge is a promise that children make to themselves, with an emphasis on trying their best, respect, listening, and diversity. It builds a foundation for all of the skills.

    page 64

* **Self-Control:** After learning the Pledge for Success, children can then learn to use their self-control to control what they do and what they say.

    page 115

* **Self-Control Time:** In order to calm down, relax, and get their self-control back, children take Self-Control Time.     page 140

* **Self-Confidence:** When children use their self-control and try their best, they give themselves the proud, happy feeling called self-confidence.

    page 166

* **Responsibility and Consequences:** With self-control and self-confidence children can take responsibility for themselves and understand the consequences of their actions.     page 193

* **Thinking and Problem Solving:** When children take responsibility and realize the consequences of their actions, they can think for themselves and problem-solve.

    page 219

* **Cooperation:** When children use their self-control, have self-confidence, take responsibility, and use their thinking and problem-solving abilities, they can cooperate with others.

    page 242

# LESSON ONE GUIDE
# THE ESSENTIALS FOR TEACHING
# THE ABCs OF LIFE

* Use positive language.

* Use varied voices in a manner consistent with your message: firm and fair, animated, and limit-setting voices.

* Provide a consistent structure with a firm "bottom line."

* Let go and put ownership back on your child.

* Teach the skills sequentially.

* Define the skills.

* Share the "whys."

* Play the games to experience the skills.

* Share the stories from yourself; then have your child share.

* Use the discussion starters to take the skills to a new level of understanding.

**To review, see The Art of Living and Working with Kids on page 29.**

# Pledge for Success
### A Promise I Make to Myself

## I will listen to what others have to say.
When I wait my turn to speak, I can hear what everyone has to say.

## I will treat others the way I would like to be treated.
Pushing, fighting, bullying, name-calling, and treating others badly hurts them and hurts me.

## I will respect the diversity of all people.
Whether we are the same or different on the outside, it's the person we are on the inside that counts.

## I will remember that I have people who care about me in my family, school, and community.
Families, like schools and communities, can be many sizes and made up of all kinds of people.

## I will try my best.
Even when I make mistakes, I learn from them. The most important thing is to keep trying.

# Self-Control

**LESSON ONE**

Self-control is when I control what I do and what I say. I use my self-control to follow directions. Using self-control helps me resist doing things that may be harmful to myself and others. Self-control helps me stay safe and be successful.

**LESSON ONE**

# Self-Control Time

Self-Control Time is a fun breathing exercise.

It helps me calm down, focus, and get my self-control back.

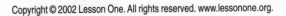

# LESSON ONE GUIDE
# HOW TO DO SELF-CONTROL TIME

* Sit up proud and relaxed wherever you may be (a couch, the floor, a chair, etc.).

* Place your feet flat on the floor in front of you. (If your feet don't reach the floor, your legs should just hang without being crossed.)

* Extend your hands palms down and place them gently on your lap. Make sure your elbows are naturally back by your sides.

* Relax your shoulders so the muscles around them are neither tight nor tense.

* Breathe deeply in through your nose and exhale through your mouth to help your body relax into this position.

* Close your eyelids lightly and continue breathing deeply.

* When using Self-Control Time as a regular part of the day, it should last approximately three minutes. When using it as a way to regain self-control, it should last approximately one minute.

# LESSON ONE GUIDE
## HOW TO HELP A CHILD REGAIN SELF-CONTROL WITH SELF-CONTROL TIME

* If a child is not using self-control, begin by reminding the child to use his or her self-control.

* If the child has not regained self-control, use your limit-setting voice and say, "Please take a Self-Control Time to get your self-control back." (Remember, the child can do Self-Control Time wherever he or she is—not in a special seat.)

* Remind the child that Self-Control Time is not a punishment, but an opportunity for the child to regain self-control.

* Have the child breathe deeply in through the nose and exhale through the mouth.

* In a firm and fair voice, calmly ask the child to open his or her eyes. Ask, "Who controls you?" Make sure the child realizes that it is up to him or her to use self-control.

* When the child is using self-control, remind the child to be proud of himself or herself for getting self-control back. Discuss with the child how Self-Control Time is a positive experience.

* This Self-Control Time lasts for approximately one minute. This differs from using Self-Control Time as a regular part of a child's day, when it lasts for approximately three minutes.

**LESSON ONE**

# Self-Confidence

Self-confidence is a proud, happy feeling I get when I have tried my best. It's up to me to be proud of myself when I have done a good job. Some ways I show myself that I have self-confidence are by sitting, standing, and speaking with pride.

# Responsibility/Consequences

**LESSON ONE**

Responsibility is when I am able to take care of myself and depend on myself. A consequence is the result of what I do and what I say. I know I am responsible for whatever consequences result from my actions.

# Thinking/Problem Solving

Thinking is when I come up with as many ideas as I can. Problem solving is when I think in order to solve a problem. I keep thinking until I solve the problem. I never give up.

# Cooperation

Cooperation is when I work well with others. I cooperate to solve problems and resolve conflicts.

# Index

For more information, please visit the Lesson One website.
www.lessonone.org